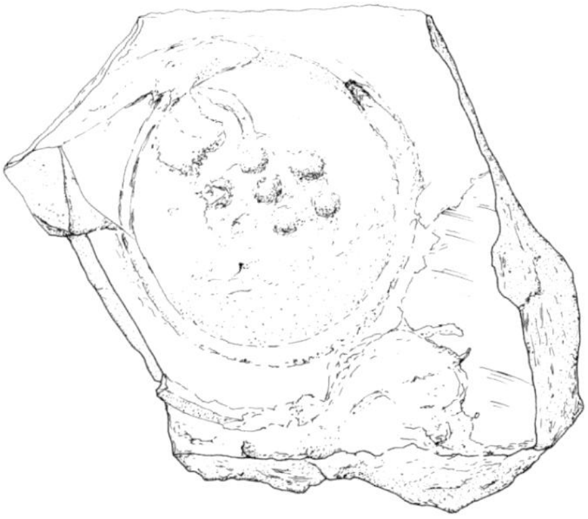

Abu Dhabi Islands Archaeological Survey

Abu Dhabi Islands Archaeological Survey

SEASON 1

G.R.D. King

An Archaeological Survey
of Ṣîr Banî Yâs, Dalmâ and Marawaḥ
(21st March to 21st April, 1992)

Published by Trident Press Ltd,
2-5 Old Bond St. London WIX 3TB
Tel: 0171 491 8770; Fax: 0171 491 8664
E-mail: tridentp@iol.ie
Internet: www.tridentpress.com

Typesetting: Johan Hofsteenge

British Library Cataloguing in Publication Data
A CIP catalogue record for this book is
available from the British Library

Published with the assistance of the
Ministry of Information and Culture,
Abu Dhabi, United Arab Emirates.

ISBN: 1900724-14-6

CONTENTS

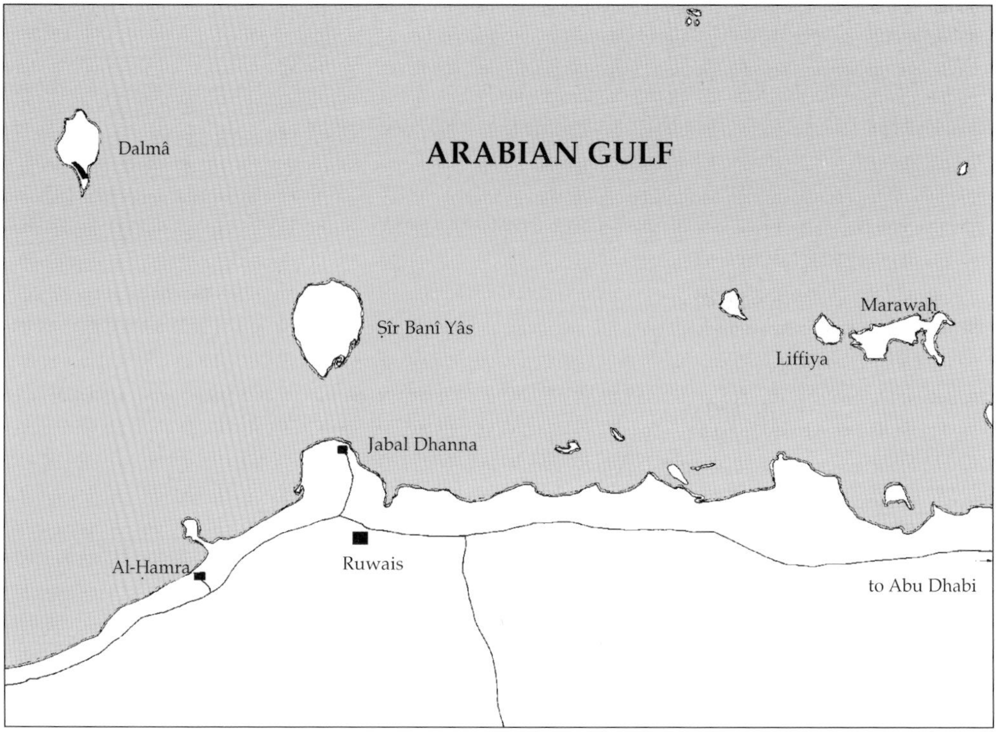

Fig. 1. Map: the Survey Area off the Western Abu Dhabi Coast.

INTRODUCTION

BETWEEN 18TH MARCH AND 20TH APRIL, 1992 the Abu Dhabi Islands Archaeological Survey (ADIAS)[1] surveyed Ṣîr Banî Yâs, Dalmâ and Marawaḥ, three offshore islands belonging to Abu Dhabi in the United Arab Emirates[2] (Fig. 1). The first season of the survey was undertaken at the request of HH Shaykh Zayed b. Sultan Al Nahyan, President of the United Arab Emirates and Ruler of Abu Dhabi and at the invitation of HE Shaykh Nahyan b. Mubarak Al Nahyan, Minister of Higher Education and Scientific Research and Chancellor of the University of the Emirates at al-ᶜAyn. HE Lieut.-General Shaykh Muhammed b. Zayed Al Nahyan kindly permitted us to survey the island of Marawaḥ.

The ADIAS project grew out of the recognition that little was known about the archaeology of the UAE islands. While an increasing amount of archaeological information has emerged elsewhere along the Gulf coast, especially on the Arabian side of the waterway, there was an almost complete lack of archaeological information regarding the offshore islands of the UAE[3]. An Iraqi team carried out excavations in 1975 on Dalmâ but no publication followed[4]. A French team, whose archaeological report was compiled by S. Cleuziou, made a general study of Dalmâ in September-October, 1979, and their comments remain the most extensive research on the archaeology of the island before it was developed and modernized[5]. On the mainland, B. Vogt and W. Tikriti carried out a survey of several coastal sites in 1983, including Bitashar, Ra's al-ᶜAysh, Jabal Dhanna (Ẓanna), Jabal Barâka, Shuwayḥât, Thumarîya, Ra's al-Qalᶜa and al-Mirfâ. This fieldwork was the only archaeological research in the region reported when the present survey commenced in 1992[6]. By contrast, palaeontology in western Abu Dhabi emirate had been far better served, with a major research programme undertaken by Dr Peter Whybrow of the Natural History Museum, London, concentrating on the mainland at Jabal Shuwayḥât and Jabal Barâka[7]. As this outline of past work indicates, little had been done on the islands of the Western Province of Abu Dhabi before 1992, and nothing had been published. Indeed, the most useful information on Ṣîr Banî Yâs and Marawaḥ available to us at the start of our fieldwork were the results of Emirates Natural History Group visits to the two islands[8].

The objective of the ADIAS team was to undertake a preliminary survey of Ṣîr Banî Yâs, Dalmâ and Marawaḥ to assess what archaeological remains existed and to report on them. It was also intended to recommend what protection should be provided where sites were threatened by development. All sites identified were described, fixed on mapping and, where appropriate, they were drawn and photographed. Pottery, flints, glass and other cultural material were collected on a selective and restricted basis to be studied for dating purposes. The ceramics retrieved will be published separately. No sondage or excavation was carried out.

Work commenced on Ṣîr Banî Yâs on Wednesday, 25th March, 1992. We had five full days in the field, departing from the island on 31st March for Dalmâ. The team was on Dalmâ from 31st March until 14th April and on Marawaḥ from 14th April. We returned to Abu Dhabi on 21st April.

Our first season of work indicates that the western areas of Abu Dhabi emirate are as important in terms of archaeology as the better known northern emirates, like Sharjah, Ajman, Umm al-Quwain, Ra's al-Khaimah and Fujairah. It also emerges in the light of this survey that the waters of the Gulf have long been a major means of communication, and the archaeological wealth of these three Abu Dhabi islands indicates that this has held true over a long period of time.

On all three islands we found evidence of antiquities stretching from the Stone Age through to the later Islamic period. Furthermore, information from local people suggests that islands apart from Ṣîr Banî Yâs, Dalmâ and Marawaḥ were settled — seasonally or permanently — in the past. We plan to examine other western Abu Dhabi islands in future seasons of ADIAS.

Notes

1 The archaeological team was based at the School of Oriental and African Studies (SOAS), University of London, and in Abu Dhabi. The team was directed by Dr G.R.D. King, Department of Art and Archaeology, SOAS and had the support of the Society for Arabian Studies, whose former Chairman, Beatrice de Cardi, OBE, was a member of the team. Other team members included Robyn Stocks, Caroline Lehmann, Fiona Baker, Joan Wucher-King and David Connally.

2 Sîr Banî Yâs is owned by HH President Shaykh Zayed b. Sultan Al Nahyan. Marawaḥ belongs to HE Lieut. General Shaykh Muhammad b. Zayed Al Nahyan. Dalmâ is administered by a branch of Abu Dhabi *baladîya*.

3 See for example, D.T. Potts, *The Arabian Gulf in Antiquity*, Oxford (1990; 1990), 2 vols.

4 B. Vogt, W. Gockel, H. Hofbauyer and A.A. Haj, "The Coastal Survey in the Western Province of Abu Dhabi, 1983", *Archaeology in the United Arab Emirates* V (1989), p. 50.

5 G. Harter, S. Cleuziou, J.P. Laffont, J. Nockin and R. Toussaint, *Emirat d'Abu Dhabi. Propositions pour Dalma* (Sept.-Oct., 1979).

6 B. Vogt, W. Gockel, H. Hofbauer and A.A. Haj, *op. cit.* V (1989), pp. 49-60.
Arabic translation by W. Tikritî, "Al maṣâḥ al-âthârî fî'l-mantiqat al-gharbîya min imârat Abû Ẓabî", *Archaeology in the United Arab Emirates* V (1989), pp. 9-19 (Arabic section).

7 P.J. Whybrow, "New stratotype; the Baynunah Formation (Late Miocene), United Arab Emirates: lithology and palaeontology", *Newsletter of Stratigraphy* 21 (1989), pp. 1-9.
P.J. Whybrow, A. Hill, W.Y. Tikriti and E.A. Hailwood, "Late Miocene primate fauna, flora and initial paleomagnetic data from the Emirate of Abu Dhabi, United Arab Emirates, *Journal of Human Evolution* 19 (1990), pp. 583-588.
P.J. Whybrow, A. Hill, W.Y. Tikriti and E.A. Hailwood, "Miocene fossils from Abu Dhabi", *Tribulus, Bulletin of the Emirates Natural History Group* (1993), 1.1, pp. 4-9.
S. McBrearty, "Lithic artifacts from Abu Dhabi's Western Region", *Tribulus, Bulletin of the Emirates Natural History Group* (1993), 3.1, pp. 4-9.

8 C.Lehmann, "Pottery Sherds, Sir Bani Yas, 2-3 May, 1991", unpublished report.
P. Hellyer (ed.), *The Natural History of Marawah Island, Abu Dhabi, United Arab Emirates. An Interim Report prepared for H.E. Major General Sheikh Mohammed Bin Zayed Al Nahyan*, Emirates Natural History Group, Abu Dhabi (June, 1990).

Acknowledgments

A remarkable level of support was brought together to sustain the ADIAS team. We are extremely grateful to HH President Shaykh Zayed b. Sultan Al Nahyan for giving his permission for the project to go ahead, for allowing us to work on Ṣîr Banî Yâs, and for receiving us on the island at the end of Ramadân. We are also very grateful to HE Lieut. General Shaykh Muhammad b. Zayed Al Nahyan for allowing us to work on Marawaḥ. We are deeply indebted to HE Shaykh Nahyan b. Mubarak Al Nahyan for his support for the project and for encouraging the idea of the survey from the first.

The team acknowledges the immense amount of work by Mr Peter Hellyer of *Emirates News* and the Chairman of Emirates Natural History Group. His sustained involvement in the project from its inception was invaluable and so too was his active encouragement of sponsorship for the project. We all remain in his debt.

Local support was generously given at Ṣîr Banî Yâs, at Dalmâ and at Marawaḥ which is greatly appreciated, and we particularly would like to thank Mr Ghassan al-Ghossain for his patience and his efficient organisation of the team's movements and accomodation on the islands. We also thank Mr Muḥammad al-Bowardi for arranging our visit to Marawaḥ. The UAE Airforce transported the team and we express our thanks to all the aircrew involved. We also express our warm thanks to Mr Eid al-Mazruʿî of the Dalmâ *baladîya* who frequently participated in our work. Mr Saʿîd al-Ghurayba and members of his family gave us a great deal of information about Dalmâ and also hospitality. Finally, we express our thanks for the support given to the project by Dr Peter Clark, formerly Director of the British Council, Abu Dhabi.

Generous assistance was given to the project by Emirates Airlines, the British Council, Abu Dhabi, the Al-Fahim Group, Abu Dhabi Company for Onshore Oil Operations (ADCO), the Union National Bank, Abu Dhabi, and Abu Dhabi National Hotel Company, Wimpey (Abu Dhabi), Spinneys, and the Higher Colleges of Technology, Abu Dhabi. Without this support, the team would have been unable to carry out the project and we express our thanks to all our sponsors.

We are grateful to Mr Sayf al-Darmaki, Director of Antiquities in Abu Dhabi for his Department's cooperation and to Dr Walid Yasin al-Tikriti for his interest and advice to the team.

The restored al-Muhannadî mosque Dalmâ, an example of the Dalmâ group of late Islamic period buildings.

ṢÎR BANÎ YÂS (SBY)

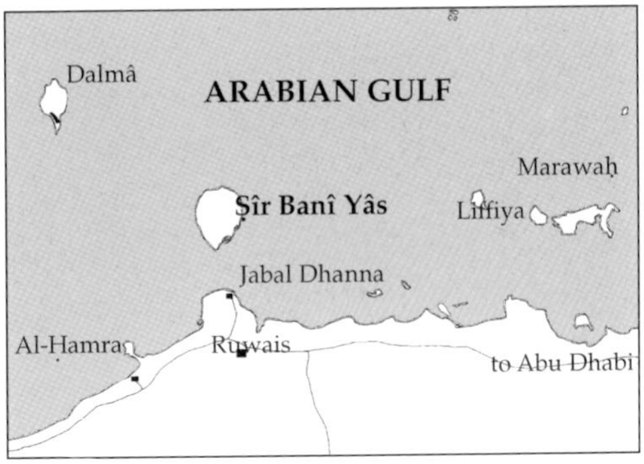

THE ISLAND OF ṢÎR BANÎ YÂS lies at UTM 663000° E/2690000° N. It is 9 kms offshore from Jabal Dhanna (Ẓanna) and 170 kms west of the capital of the United Arab Emirates, Abu Dhabi[1]. The island is 17.5 kms from north to south and 9 kms from east to west, with a range of bare volcanic mountains in the central area rising to a height of 148 m.

Apart from a salty well in the area of the present-day workers' camp in the SE of the island (at Khawr Daʿsa, the Meriton Bay of British mariners), there is now no permanent natural water supply on the island, and only occasional rain pools seem to have been used in the recent past. However, a spring is marked on mapping on the east side of the island[2]. Ṣîr Banî Yâs is a major wild animal sanctuary, and access to the island is restricted. The coastal plain has been heavily planted with trees over the past 20 years as a result of HH Shaykh Zayed's interest in afforestation. Fences around the planted areas protect the trees from the very large herds of gazelle that roam free on the island. There are herds of oryx, llamas, ostrich, rhea, giraffe and numerous other species of animals and birds which have been introduced by order of the President.

Plate 1. The central mountains, Ṣîr Banî Yâs.

The coast of Ṣîr Banî Yâs has been transformed by landfill operations and dredging over the last two decades, and earlier maps no longer reflect the present geographical reality. Nevertheless, areas were identified where the original landscape and shoreline survive intact. For example, at the north end of the island near Ra's Danân, earlier shorelines are clearly visible descending in terraces towards the present coast.

The village of al-Ẓahir at the north end of Ṣîr Banî Yâs was already in ruins by 1932, and some decades ago the population moved to the island of Dalmâ to the north-west. The vanished village at ʿAwâfî on the south-west coast of the island was probably contemporaneous to judge by pottery from the nearby pearling beach (Site SBY 32). We have not established when ʿAwâfî was abandoned. Those living on the island in 1992 were connected with the residence of Shaykh Zayed, with dredging operations, animal husbandry or the plantations.

Accounts of Ṣîr Banî Yâs are few. The earliest reference to the island seems to date to 1590, when Gasparo Balbi, a Venetian who was jeweller to the Republic of Venice, recorded "Sirbeniast" as one of the places among the islands off whose coasts pearls were fished[3].

The islands off Abu Dhabi came into clearer light in the early decades of the 19th century as the East Indian Company sent survey vessels into the Gulf to explore its waters. A number of reports and maps emerged, giving the first accurate recording of the islands, with special attention given to Ṣîr Banî Yâs.

Captain Robert Taylor described the coast of the Banî Yâs in 1818, mentioning the "Kiran Beniyas", the ports lying between Sharjah and Qaṭar, but although he describes their fishing and pearling, nothing is said of Ṣîr Banî Yâs island itself[4]. However, it is in the following years that Ṣîr Banî Yâs became known to British navigators in the Gulf: according to a British report of 1823, Suwaidan b. Zaʿal moved there in November, 1822[5]:

> *In November last he proceeded to Muscat, when he received some presents from the Imaum, and since his return he has I hear gone to establish himself in the Island of Seer Beniyas which is the Southern-most of the group lately discovered, and is described by Captain Grubb in his report of the 19th September 1821. He is accompanied by his friend and relation Shaikh Nuhaiman; they have nearly a thousand men at their command and possess one fine Batille and about fifty fishing Boats.*

Between 1820 and 1829 survey of the Arabian coast by the East Indian Company navy produced detailed accounts of Ṣîr Banî Yâs itself and the waters off it, as well as other islands in the area (Fig. 2) and a water-colour was made by Dr Maskell of the island in 1822 (Fig. 3)[6]. As a result of this attention by navy hydrographers, by *ca* 1823, Ṣîr Banî Yâs had appeared in more populist mapping of Arabia available to the public at large[7].

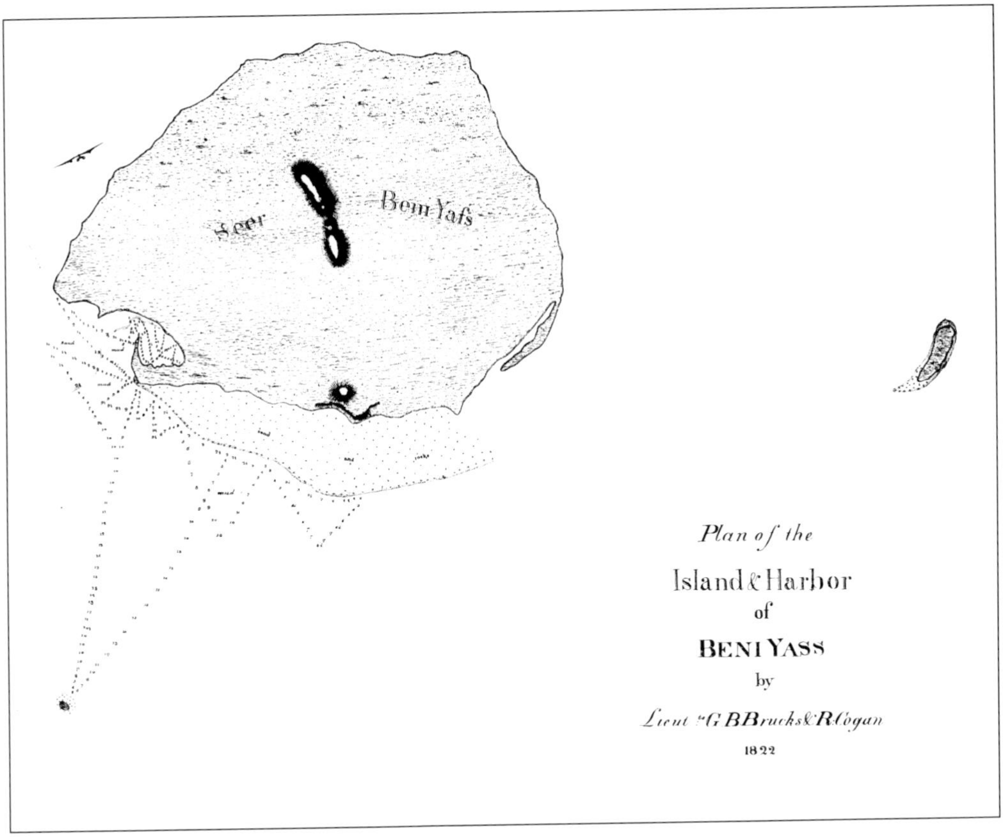

Fig. 2. "Plan of the Island and Harbor of Beni Yass by Lieuts. G.B.Brucks & R. Cogan, 1822" (India Office Library and Records, ORW 1990a 1379, Chart 8).

During the initial exploration of Gulf waters by the British in the 1820s, the islands on the Arabian side, were examined by Captain Maude on HMS *Favourite* (including Ṣîr Banî Yâs) who made the following notes[8]:

Geziret Beni Aass is in lat. 24" 34' north, and long. 52" 40' east. It is rather high in the centre, very rugged, and extending to the south-west in a low point, which nearly joins the main land, leaving a narrow channel, navigable by small boats only. The Arabian coast, to the westward of this, is very low, and the pilot stated that there were several small islands off it, but he considered them dangerous to be approached, except by boats. The channel between Arzeneeah and Gezirat Beni Aass is perfectly safe[9].

A further description of the island is provided by Captain Brucks, published in 1856:

SEER BANIYAS ISLAND
The entrance to the cove is in lat. 24° 15' 10" N., long. 52° 46' 50" E. This island is rather high, having a peak in the centre; is seventeen miles in circumference, and appears of volcanic origin. On the southern side is a small cove [Khawr Daʿsa or Meriton Bay], with five fathoms of water in it, and three fathoms in the entrance[10].

He continues with details of how best to approach the island and to avoid its shallows and reefs, and warns against the rapidity of the tidal flow between the island and the mainland.

An account of the island also appears in the *The India Directory* of 1891 with revised co-ordinates[11]:

> *SEIR BENU YAS, situated 6 leagues to the S.E. by E. of Dalmah, has two peaked hills in the centre of the island, 430 ft. high, in lat. 24° 19′ N., lon. 52° 37′ E. It is about 6 m. in extent, N. and S., and 3 to 4 m. in breadth, its N.W. extremity terminating in a low sandy point. It is bounded on its N. and E. side by a shoal-bank extending 1 or 2 m. from the shore. The S. point of the island is distant about 3 m. from the main land, leaving a narrow shoal channel, navigable only by small pearl boats. The S.E. point of the island curves round to the W., forming a safe land-locked harbour within it, for small vessels, with 5 and 6 fathoms water, and from 3 to 4 fathoms at the entrance. The channel between Arzanah and Seir Benu Yas is safe, with irregular depths from 8 to 19 fathoms. From hence, the whole coast to the W. is very low, and several small islands lie off it, considered dangerous to approach.*

The same source erroneously conflates Jabal Dhanna and Ra's al-Mughayraq south of Ṣîr Banî Yâs, reporting it as "Jebel Duwarikah".

J.G. Lorimer also describes the island in the early years of this century[12]:

> *YÂS*
> *An island in the bay between Abu Dhabi and Qatar; it lies rather over 100 miles west by south of Abu Dhabi Town, 18 miles east-south-east of the island of Dalmah and only 4 or 5 miles north of the coast of Dhafrah at Jabal Dhannah. The island measures 6½ miles from north to south by 5 miles across,*

and its shape is roughly oval with a remarkable indentation at its south end. The shores of Yâs are low, but the centre consists of volcanic hills culminating in twin peaks each 430 feet high. The indentation already mentioned forms a singular landlocked natural harbour, to British mariners known as Meriton Bay [Khawr Daʿsa]; the depth is from 4-6 fathoms and the bottom mud, but the entrance is rather narrow and inconvenient. The island is frequented in winter by Bani Yas fishermen, mostly from Dhafrah, and pearl boats sometimes take refuge there during storms. The following pearl banks exist in the neighbourhood: -- Ghashshah, 3 miles north of the north-west corner of the island; Umm-al-Kurkum, 3 miles north of the north-east corner; Buwairdah, 5 miles to the south-west; and Dhahr-al-Yâs, which, though 33 miles to the westward and considerably nearer to Dalmah, appears to take its name from Yâs Island. Water is obtainable only after rain. Yâs is included in the Abu Dhabi Principality of Trucial 'Omân.

Fig. 3. "Seer Beni Yass, distant 6¼ miles" (1822), by Dr Maskell (India Office Library and Records, ORW 1990a 1379, view 49)

The island is mentioned in *The Persian Gulf Pilot* of 1932[13] under the name "Jezirat Yas" with "Sir Bani Yas" as an alternative. There were the remains of a village on the NE coast of the island, obviously al-Ẓahir, although the name is not mentioned. It is stated clearly that the village was in ruins, although it is not explained whether it was deserted or not. Meriton Bay is described as an almost circular basin, completely sheltered, and with a maximum depth of 11 m., although anchorage in the bay for sailing vessels was not recommended because of the strong tidal streams.

From 1966, the British Royal Air Force used the island as a live firing range for British and local military forces[14]. In the course of the survey and subsequent excavation we have found a great deal of evidence of shells and shrapnel from this period.

Plate 2. The sabkha *at Jabal Dhanna.*

In a report on a survey in the western areas of Abu Dhabi emirate, Dr B. Vogt refers to three archaeological sites at Ṣîr Banî Yâs and Jabal Dhanna, marked imprecisely on a map published in 1975 by the Department of Antiquities and Tourism at al-ᶜAyn. This report seems to derive from the unpublished archaeological investigations by an Iraqi team carried out in 1975[15].

Before our survey began, Carolyn Lehmann gave us notes made during a visit by the Emirates Natural History Group (ENHG) to Ṣîr Banî Yâs on 2-3 May, 1991[16]. These drew attention to several archaeological sites including ceramics noted at the llama pens on the eastern side of the island and an "old house" which was tentatively recognized as a mosque.

Peter Hellyer also informed the writer of sites that he had noted during the ENHG visit in May 1991, including old houses, a graveyard and a rainwater tank in plantations in the northern part of the island and attributed to the Islamic period. He also referred to what had seemed to be pre-Islamic graves on the northern bluffs[17].

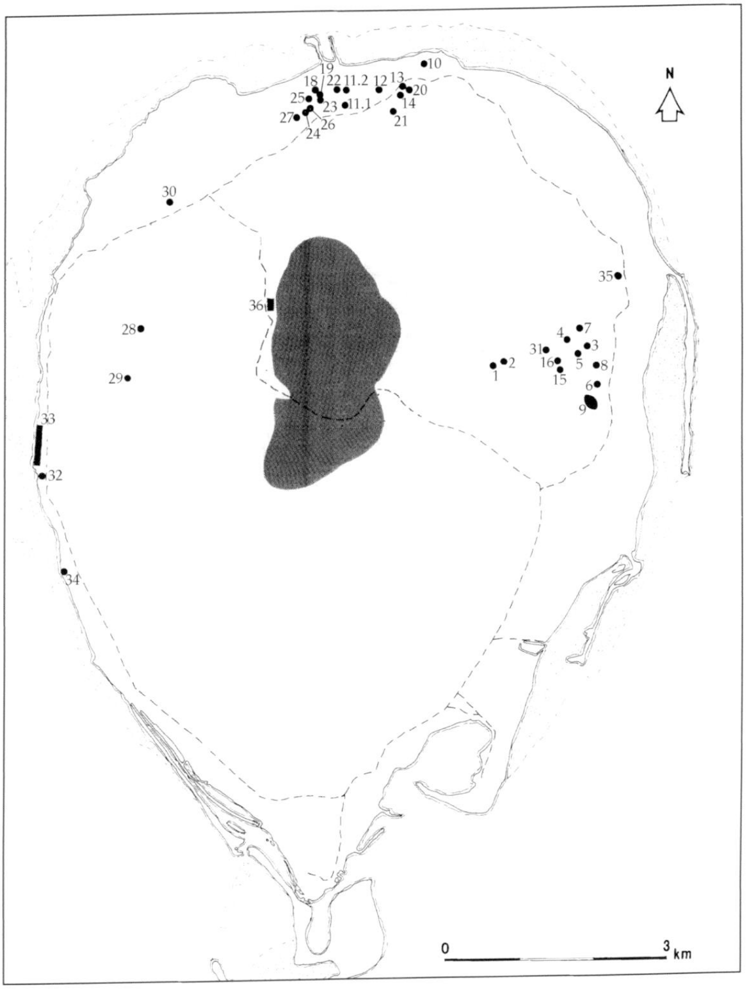

Fig. 4. Ṣîr Banî Yâs: Site locations.

THE SITES[18]

Date: 25.3.92 **Figs:** 4, 5. **Type:** Pottery scatter **Period:** *ca* 6th-7th C. AD

SBY 1.1 & 1.2

Site SBY 1.1 was a dense pottery scatter on a ridge above al-Khawr. Site SBY 1.2 was a smaller pottery scatter on the ridge a little further east. SBY 1.1 extended *ca* 30 m. x 30 m. Both were due east of Sites SBY 2.1 and 2.2 were on the slope of a low, sandy, flint covered ridge which runs NW/SE. The ridge was approximately 2-3 m. high. A track ran across the ridge on an east-west alignment and most of the pottery was located to the south of this track. Tabular and nodular flint was concentrated on the ridge, in higher density than elsewhere on the plateau. Water erosion had created several slight gulleys with the erosion more marked on the SW side of the site. Gazelles tend to concentrate in herds in this area of the island and there was disturbance in places caused by gazelles scratching through the sand to bedrock.

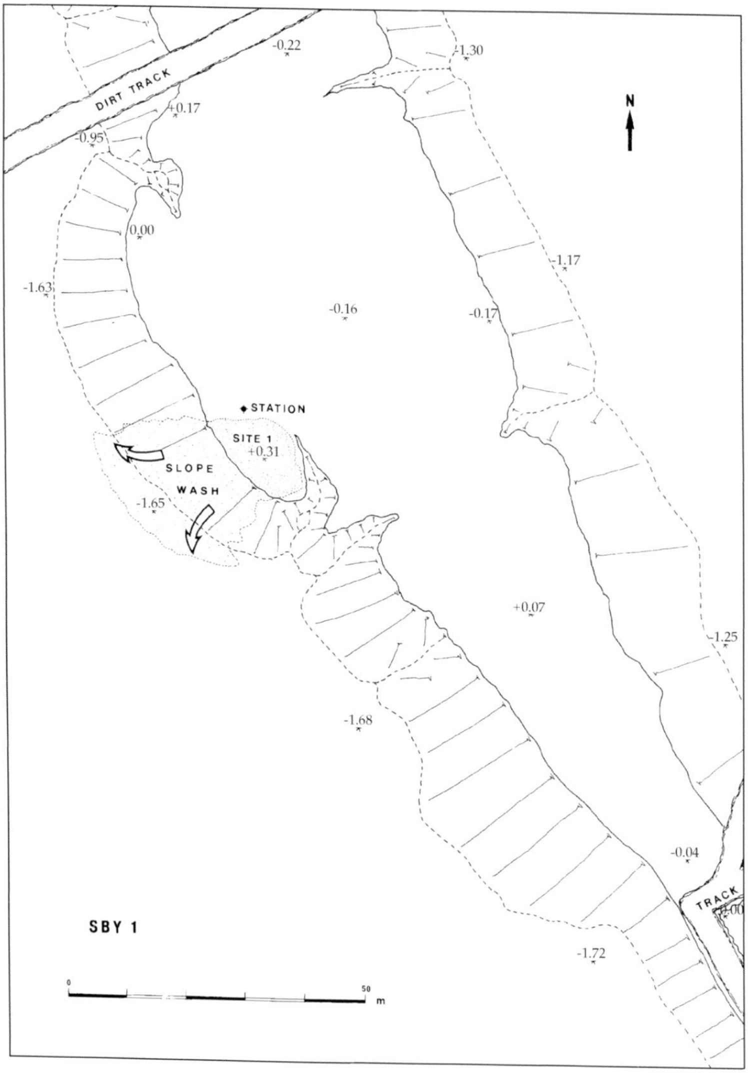

Fig. 5. *Ṣîr Banî Yâs: Site SBY 1.*

No structural remains were visible but a possible slight mound was discerned. The sherd scatter ran westwards down the slope, suggesting that the sherds may have eroded out. We associate the *ca* 6th-7th C. AD ceramics from this area with those found at Sites SBY 2.1 and 2.2.

SBY 2.1

Date: 25.3.92 **Figs:** 4, 6. **Type:** Structure **Period:** *ca* 6th-7th C. AD

A large, low and irregular mound (*ca* 50 m. N-S, 34 m. E-W; 3 m. high) of broken flints, grey stone and brown sand, which lies 50 m. west of site 1. The central area of the mound appeared to have been redeposited by bulldozing. If it was a structure, the plan was not readily discernible. There were traces of light grey plaster and pottery found at the site. There was a general scatter of finds away from the site in all directions, overlapping with Site SBY 2.2 which, for the moment, we treated as separate.

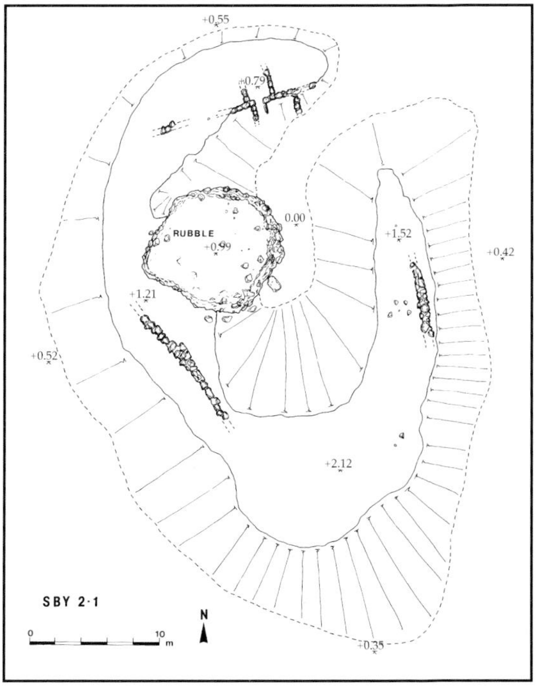

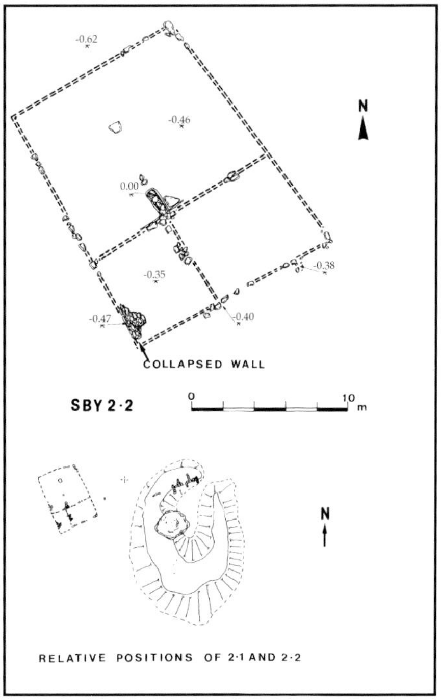

Date: 25.3.92 **Figs:** 4, 5. **Type:** Pottery scatter **Period:** *ca* 6th-7th C. AD

SBY 2.2

Site SBY 2.2 was a smaller mound standing on level ground 20 m. to the NW of SBY 2.1. It was approximately 1 m.-2 m. high with several wall sections visible above the ground surface, partly hidden by debris, one of which seemed to be a door jamb. The walls were constructed of irregular, medium sized stones, some of which were cut from the substrata. They were bonded by light grey/brown mortar. A smooth light grey plaster, 1 cm thick, covered some areas of the walls. It probably relates to the disturbed SBY 2.1.

Top left: Fig. 6. Ṣîr Banî Yâs: Site SBY 2.1.
Top right: Fig. 7. Ṣîr Banî Yâs: Site SBY 2.2.

Plate 3. Plastered door jamb (SBY 2.2), Ṣîr Banî Yâs.

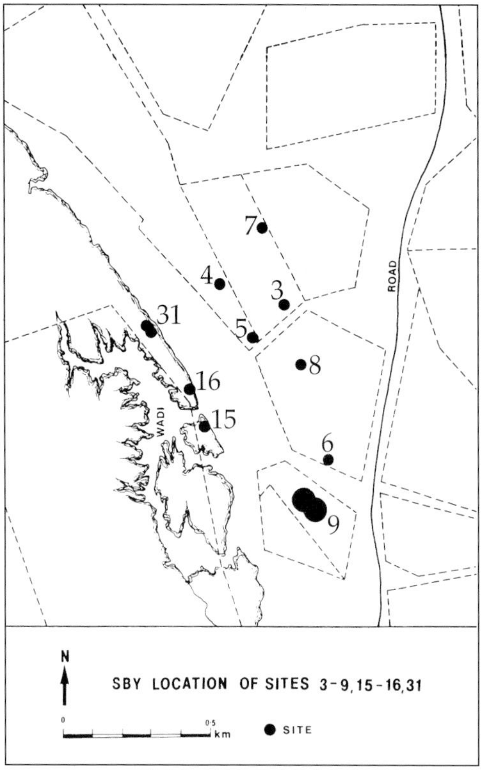

Fig. 8. Ṣîr Banî Yâs: Location of sites SBY 3-9, 15-16 and 31.

Sites SBY 3-9

Sites SBY 3-9 were situated on the coastal plain north of Jabal Buwaytir, in the al-Khawr area, and at the foot of the last ridge descending eastwards towards the shore from the central mountains. For sites SBY 3-9 inclusive, see Fig. 8: Distribution map. Sites SBY 3-SBY 6 were within the llama pens while Sites SBY 7-9 lay further south in enclosures.

Plate 4. Courtyard house (SBY 3), Ṣîr Banî Yâs.

SBY 3

Date: 25.3.92 **Figs:** 4, 8, 9. **Type:** Courtyard house **Period:** *ca* 6th-7th C. AD

Site SBY 3 was situated in llama pen 4 on level ground. It consisted of a low mound of light brown sandy soil and medium large stones to the west. The surface had been churned by llama treadage. It measured 10.5 m. x 9.8 m., and was approximately 1 m. high. Around this mound on three sides (north, east and south) were traces of stone walling,

Plate 5. Plaster fragment from courtyard house (SBY 3), Ṣîr Banî Yâs.

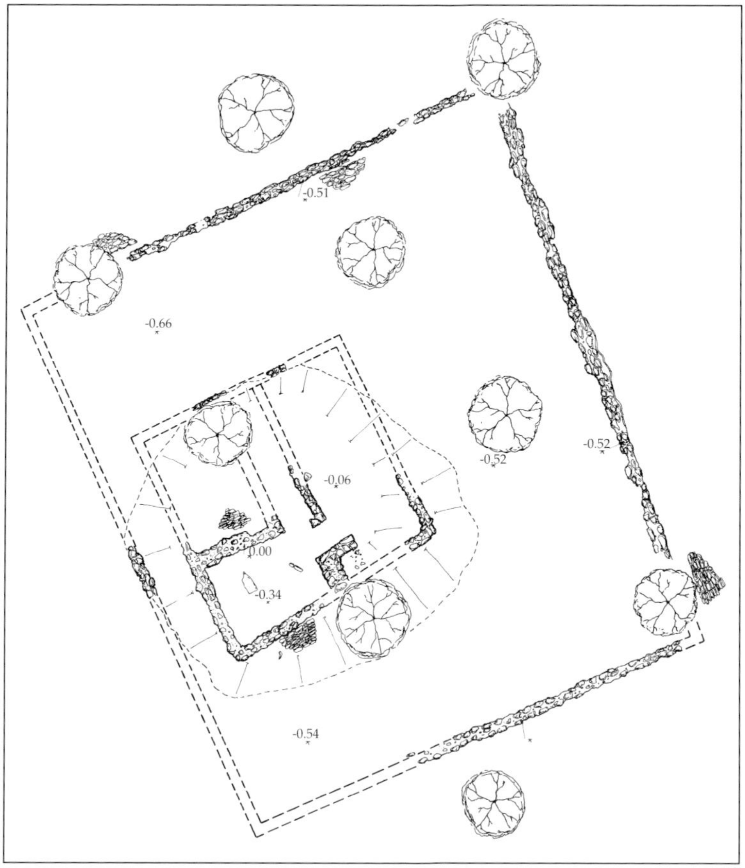

Fig. 9. Ṣîr Banî Yâs: Site SBY 3.1.

surviving to no more than 30 cms above present ground level. The walls were aligned to the compass and they were of medium-large rough pieces of stone, mostly grey and coarse. The mortar was brown and sandy. There were also remains of a hard, pinkish-white plaster attached to the walls and fallen plaster. It seemed very likely that the internal and the external faces of the walls were once plastered. Finds included tabular flint and brown stone, several pieces of architectural stone and pottery.

Site SBY 3.2 was a small *ca* 6th-7th C. pottery scatter approximately 102 m. to the west and north of a small shed to the NW of Site SBY 3.

Site SBY 3.3 was a small *ca* 6th-7th C. AD pottery scatter covering about 10 m^2., just inside the gate of llama pen 4, to the south of Site SBY 3.

Date: 25.3.92 **Figs:** 4, 8, 9. **Type:** Courtyard house **Period:** *ca* 6th-7th C. AD

SBY 4

Site SBY 4 was a rectangular mound on level ground in the NE part of llama pen 4. It was 16 m. x 14 m., and 1-2 m. high with large and small grey stone rubble from coarse beach rock, brown sandy soil and small white stones. Stones were medium-large, *ca* 40 cms x 30 cms x 15 cms.There was also a light grey-white plaster, 1 cm thick, which coated some surfaces. Samples of decorated plaster were also located. The limits

Plate 6. Courtyard house (SBY 4), Ṣîr Banî Yâs.

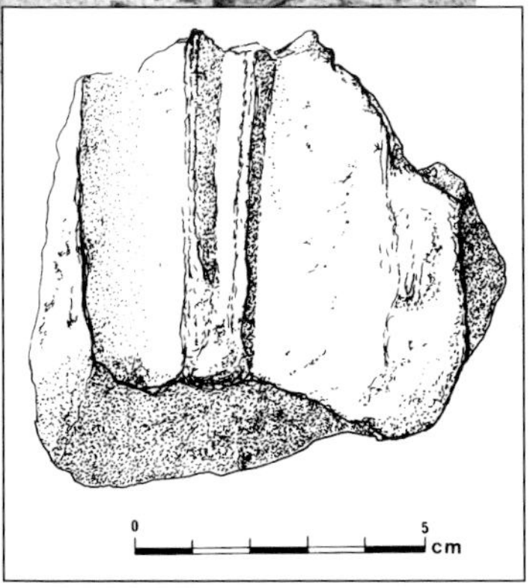

Fig. 10. Ṣîr Banî Yâs: Plaster fragment from Site SBY 4.

of this mound were enclosed by the remains of outer wall footings. The mound also preserved traces of the stone footings of structures, showing the same construction technique as the outer wall traces. A room was identified at the SE corner, approximately 8.3 m. x 4.8 m. externally and 5.5 m. x 2.5 m. internally. To NE and SE were smaller rectangular rooms adjoining the courtyard on the north side. Site SBY 4 may have been a more complex building than Site SBY 3.1, to which the mound was comparable.

SBY 5

Date: 25.3.92 **Figs:** 4, 8. **Type:** Courtyard house? **Period:** *ca* 6th-7th C. AD

Site SBY 5 was a sub-oval mound on level ground, consisting of soil and stones measuring approximately 9 m. x 9 m. and 1.5 m. high. It was at the SE corner of llama pen 4. There was a great deal of disturbance due to planting and fencing. Its walls were aligned to the compass. The mound had been partly cut away by a track to the south of the pen. The structural remains were of grey beach stone, some roughly cut, and measuring 40 cms x 26 cms x 10 cms. They were carefully laid to form what we took to be walls. The N/S wall was approximately 60 cms wide. A square (rectangular?) plastered "room" was identified to the east within the rubble. The "room" measured 2.3 m. x 1.9 m. The plaster on the

Plate 7. Courtyard house (SBY 5), Ṣîr Banî Yâs.

interior surfaces was approximately 1 cm thick, light grey and coarse with occasional tiny white pebbles. To the west of the room were indications of other walls.

Date: 26.3.92 **Figs:** 4, 8. **Type:** Courtyard house **Period:** *ca* 6th-7th C. AD **SBY 6**

Site 6 was an irregular mound on flat land gently rising on the south side. The mound continued to the SE, and lay partly outside the fence of the pen where it had been disturbed by the motor track beside the fence. The stone was grey crystalline beach rock with occasional chalky stones.

Plate 8. Courtyard house (SBY 6), Ṣîr Banî Yâs.

It stood 1 m. high, measuring overall 18 m. x 20 m. To the NE and to the NW, traces of an enclosure wall appeared above ground-level, but it was largely masked by sand and bushes. Within the enclosure wall were the remains of a building measuring 14 m. x 11 m. In the central south area there were remains of the footing of stone walling, but only small areas of true stone coursing were visible. One wall in the central mound near the fence on the south side measured 30 cms. in width, built of neatly fitting stones, cut to shape on the face of the wall. There appeared to be traces of a brown sandy mortar that had been largely washed away. A light-grey white plaster appeared on the interior faces of wall surfaces in the central mound. To the NE and partly to NW was an enclosure wall just above ground level, but the evidence for this was very patchy because of concealing sand and bushes. One wall in the central mound beside the track was 30 cms wide and built of neatly fitting stones, cut to shape on the face.

SBY 7

Date: 26.3.92 **Figs:** 4, 8. **Type:** Courtyard house **Period:** *ca* 6th-7th C. AD

In the north part of llama pen 4 on the east side of the enclosure and on level ground was yet another occupation mound, measuring 24 m. x 20 m. overall, although the structural mound was 16 m. x 14 m. with gently sloping sides. It rose to a maximum of 1.5 m. The mound consisted of grey stone, soil and sand with the walls of buildings just exposed on the north and south side. The wall on the north side was 60 cms wide.

To the north, east and west was an enclosing courtyard, the remains of whose stone walls were just perceptible above the surface sand.

Plate 9. Possible courtyard house (SBY 7), Ṣîr Banî Yâs.

Date: 26.3.92 **Figs:** 4, 8. **Type:** ? **Period:** *ca* 6th-7th C. AD **SBY 8**

Site 8 was a low mound of soil, grey beach stones and sand set on flat ground in the pen immediately south of llama pen 4. The mound was approximately 14 m. x 12 m. and 1 m. in height, with irregular sloping sides. The site was too indistinct and damaged to define any structural form and no courtyard walls were obvious. There was minimal pottery on and near the site.

Date: 26.3.92 **Figs:** 4, 8. **Type:** Occupation mound **Period:** *ca* 6th-7th C. AD **SBY 9.1-9.3**

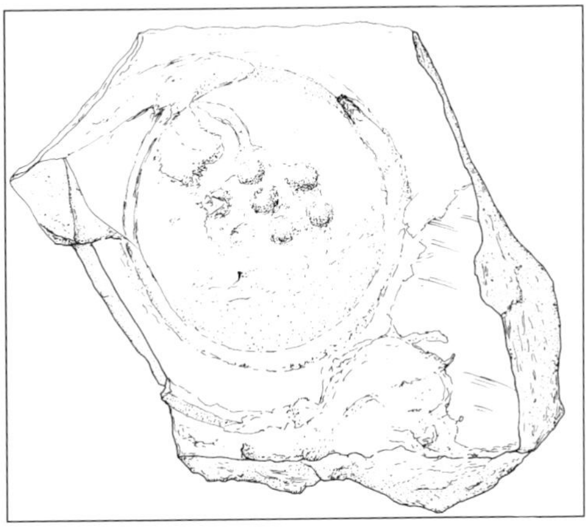

Site 9 was a low flattened occupation mound approximately 220 m. x 160 m. reaching 1.5 m. - 2 m. in height above the surrounding ground surface. It sloped down eastwards from the higher ground to the west.

The mound was a mixture of light brown sandy soil with numerous small to medium pieces of stone, mostly grey beach rock. Occasional flint nodules and tile flint were noted. The surface appeared to have been severely disturbed by machinery during preparation for the plantations. Despite disturbance to the surface, concentrations of pottery were found and a block of decorative plaster with a vine scroll in relief was recovered from the surface (Plate 10). Ceramics suggested a *ca* 6th-7th C. AD date.

Site SBY 9.2 was part of Site 9.1. It was a narrow area to the south of 9.1 beside the southern fence of the plantation. Pottery, flint and plaster was

Fig. 11-13. Ṣîr Banî Yâs: Plaster fragments from Site SBY 9.

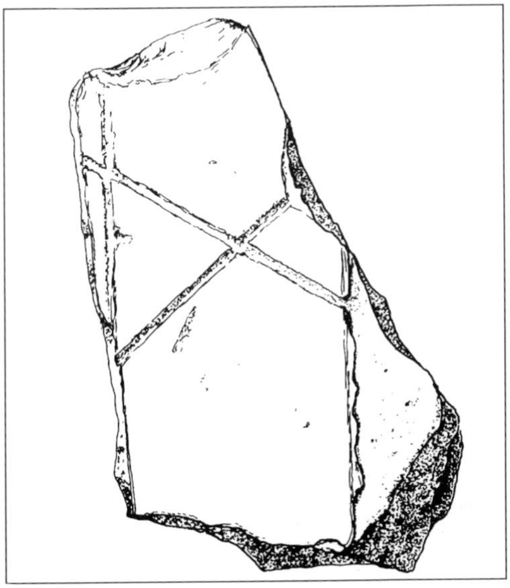

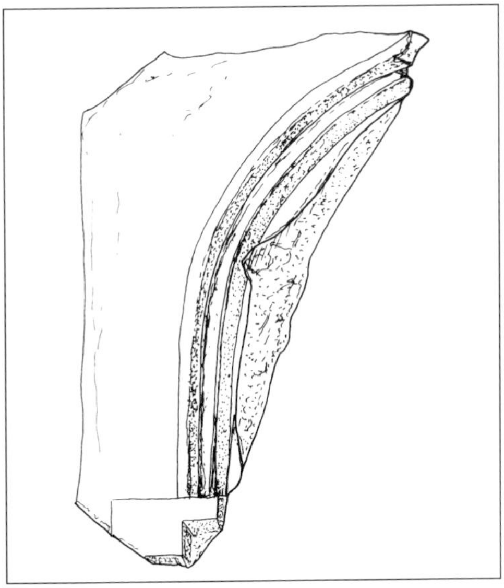

cms.

concentrated in an area measuring 40 m. x 2 m. Artefacts were probably dragged from Site 9.1 during levelling.

Site SBY 9.3 was a flat area with occasional pottery scatters covering an area of approximately 60 m^2; the pottery was probably material from Site 9.1, disturbed when the tree plantations were established.

Plate 10 (opposite). Decorated plaster from Site SBY 9.1; ca 6th-7th C. A.D.

Sites SBY 10-27

This group of sites was concentrated in the northern part of Ṣîr Banî Yâs, on the old shore-line near Ra's Danân, the deserted village of al-Ẓahir (al-Thahir) and on the ridges behind Ra's Danân. There has been disturbance to the sites by plantations and by the extension work to the shoreline through dredging and filling. This has been particularly the case with the sites around al-Ẓahir. The ridges to the west of al-Ẓahir, closer to Ra's Danân, were still remarkably well preserved and undisturbed.

This group of sites extended chronologically from the Late Stone Age through to the later Islamic period.

Date: 26.3.92 **Figs:** 4, 14. **Type:** Mosque **Period:** Late Islamic **SBY 10**

Site 10 was a mosque within a plantation enclosure in the Bûṭabr area: the mosque was said by people from Dalmâ to be 300 years old. It was surrounded by a low mound formed by wind-blown sand. A rectangular building measuring 9.40 m. x 4.00 m. externally, the walls were 0.5 cms thick, but the badly broken walls of the *miḥrâb* were 0.07 cms thick, and its maximum height above the ground surface was 0.8 m. There was no reason to suppose that the walls ever rose much, if at all, above their present height and there was never any built superstructure. The mosque was constructed of beach rock, with a quasi-herringbone construction. No mortar bonding was visible in the walls, although it may have been eroded away, for the gravel and broken shells around the walls suggested mortar washout. Nor does any plaster or mortar facing remain on the walls.

The single entrance to the mosque was in the centre of the east wall, opposite the *miḥrâb* in the centre of the west (*qibla*) wall. The *miḥrâb* formed a projection in the centre of the *qibla* wall at 280°, forming a curve on the exterior and a square on the interior: it was constructed of particularly large distinctive panels cut from beach-rock.

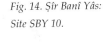

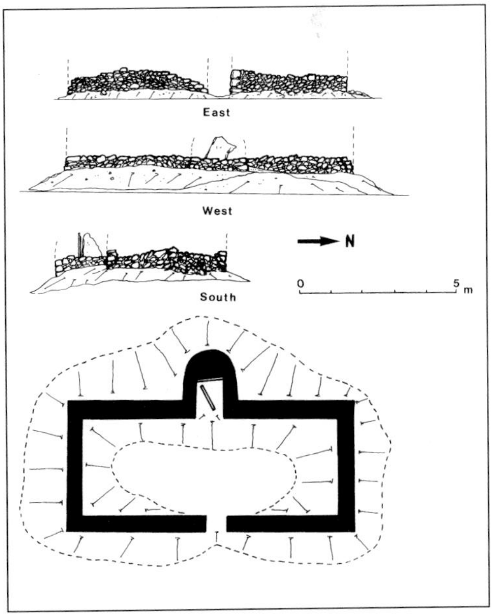

Fig. 14. Ṣîr Banî Yâs: Site SBY 10.

Plate 11. Mosque (SBY 10), Ṣîr Banî Yâs.

SBY 11.1

Date: 26.3.92 **Figs:** 4. **Type:** Cemetery **Period:** Late Islamic

This site was a late Islamic period cemetery with 45 graves and three possible graves. It was in a plantation north and east of the road, and 400 m. W. of the SW corner of an old established palm grove, al-Nakhayl. The landscape in this area had undergone immense change because of land-fill and coastline extensions. The cemetery originally would have been on a coastal beach, but it is now inland because of land reclamation. It was generally undisturbed, especially at the southern end. The graves were typical of the Islamic graves of the region, with a head and a foot stone and a kerb made of large stones. The kerbed enclosure of each grave was filled with stones varying in size between quite large tile flint slabs (*ca* 40 cms x 20 cms) to small rocks (*ca* 8 cms x 6 cms or 3 cms. x 5 cms).

The graves varied in their elaborateness. Some had well defined kerbs and a cairn within the kerb enclosure: others had only head and foot stones.

SBY 11.2

Date: 26.3.92 **Figs:** 4, 15. **Type:** Cemetery **Period:** Late Islamic

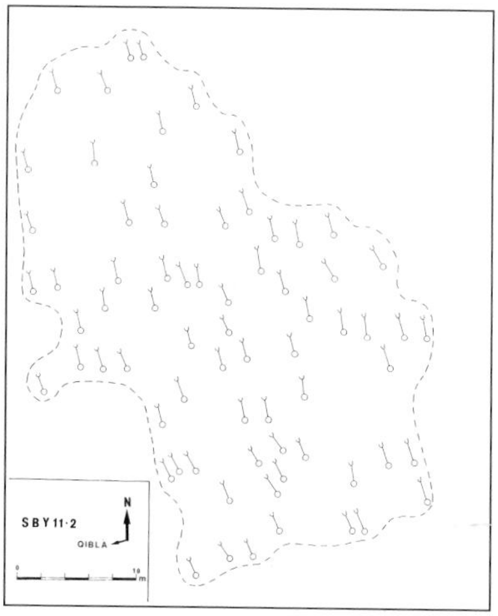

This site was another late Islamic period cemetery lying 290 m. north of Site SBY 11.1 but probably of the same general period. It had 71 graves and measured 45 m. N-S x 40 m. E-W. The graves were oriented to *qibla* at 255°-260° and were akin to those at Site SBY 11.1. Again, it was once on the shoreline before recent land-fill operations. The graves had the usual head/foot stones of about 20 cms.

There was a sherd scatter throughout the graveyard which was associated with the neighbouring Site SBY 22 village settlement.

Fig. 15.

Date: 27.3.92 **Figs:** 4, 16. **Type:** Cistern **Period:** Before 1357/1938 **SBY 12**

Site SBY 12 was a rectangular cistern measuring 3.18 m. x 2.20 m. situated in the old, well-established palm-grove of al-Nakhayl. The cistern was originally part of an irrigation system serving the grove. It was repaired in *Ṣafar*, 1357/April, 1938 with cement, and bore an inscription incised into the cement:
"*Ṣafar* 1357. Its owner is Ṣaqr b. Muhammad al-Muraykhî".

Plate 12. Cistern (SBY 12), Ṣîr Banî Yâs.

The al-Muraykhî family used to be engaged in the pearl trade[19]. The Muraykhî Mosque and Pearl House at Dalmâ are named after this family and were founded by Muḥammad Jâsim al-Muraykhî.

Running along the east side of the palm-grove was a sea-stone and coral wall. It seemed very likely that this was re-used stone from the village of al-Ẓahir, immediately to the east.

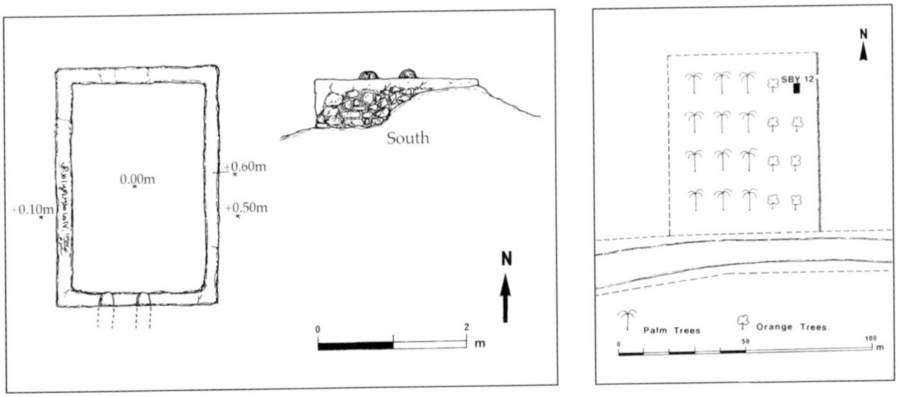

Fig. 16. Ṣîr Banî Yâs: Site SBY 12.

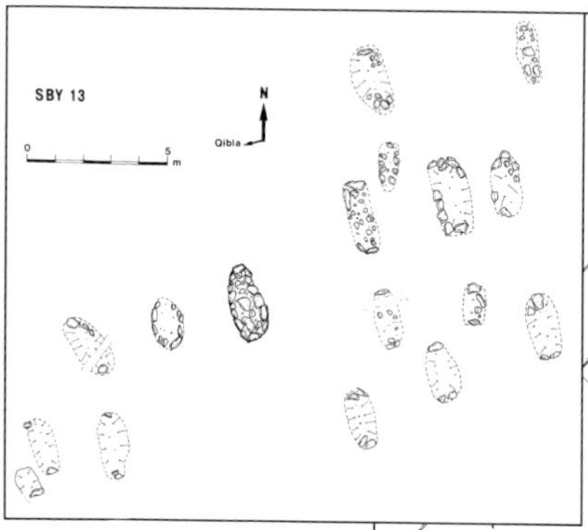

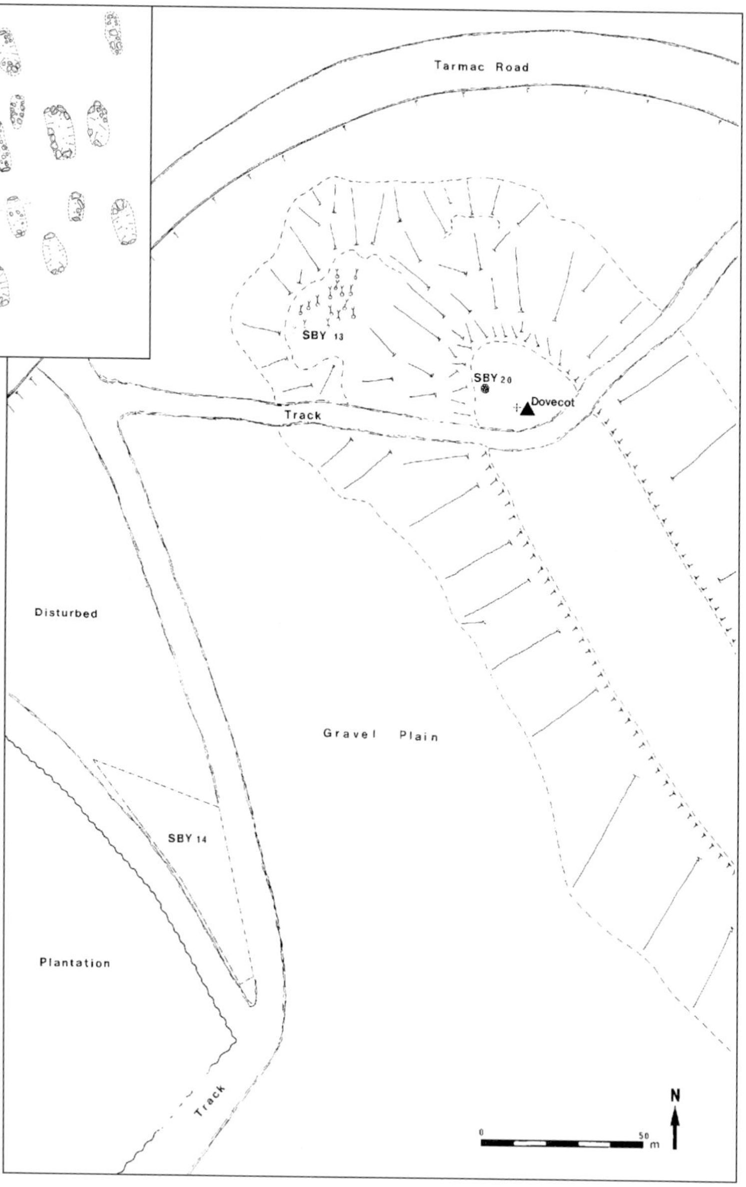

Fig. 17. Ṣîr Banî Yâs: Site SBY 13.

Fig. 18. Ṣîr Banî Yâs: Location of Sites SBY 13, 14, 20.

SBY 13

Date: 26.3.92 **Figs:** 4, 17, 18. **Type:** Cemetery **Period:** Late Islamic

This was a group of 17 Islamic period graves lying NW of a dovecot on a prominent eminence on the eastern side of the island.

SBY 14

Date: 26.3.92 **Figs:** 4, 18, 19. **Type:** Settlement **Period:** Late Islamic

See also Site SBY 21

This was a destroyed village, *ca* 210 m. west of prominent white dovecot beside Site SBY 13, set on an eminence. There were wall traces north of

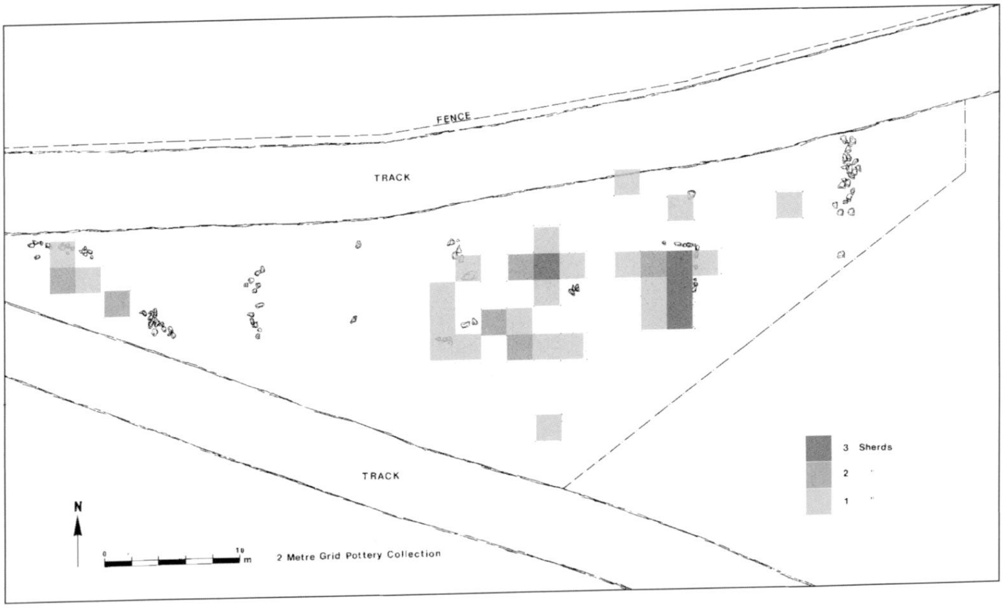

Fig. 19. Ṣîr Banî Yâs: Site SBY 14. Ceramic distribution.

a track running westwards and outlines of walls and house platforms could be identified but nothing remained in elevation. Two major groupings of houses were recognized.

SBY 15

Date: 26.3.92 **Figs:** 4, 8. **Type:** Stone cairn **Period:** Unknown.

The site stood close to the edge of the ridge that lies immediately west of the llama pens at Khawr al-Janûbî. It was immediately south of the track from the pens. It was a circular cairn of stones approximately 2 m./2.2 m. in diameter, with a maximum height of 50 cms. Stones were loose in the centre, and had spread and flattened with collapse. Two pieces of weathered, red, unglazed pottery with a black core were found in the immediate vicinity of the cairn but they were not removed.

Plate 13. Stone cairn (SBY 15), Ṣîr Banî Yâs.

SBY 16 **Date:** 27.3.92 **Figs:** 4, 8. **Type:** Circle of stones **Period:** Unknown.

The site stood close to the edge of the ridge that lies immediately west of the llama pens at Khawr al-Janûbî: it was *ca* 25 m. north of the track that ran up from the pens, and N/NE of Site 15. It was an oval ring of flat black-brown flint tiles, very irregular and loose, measuring 1.7 m. x 1.1 m. and reaching a maximum height of 30 cms. It may have been a recent hide. There were no finds.

SBY 18[20]

The various elements of SBY 18.1-18.9 were associated with campsites situated on a terrace overlooking the coast at Ra's Danân at the northern end of Ṣîr Banî Yâs: the sites overlooked SBY 19 in the sand filled gulley to the west. Site SBY 22, the abandoned village of al-Ẓahir, lay to the east of site SBY 18. Sites SBY 18.1-18.9, like site SBY 19, have evidence of use in the Late Stone Age and the Late Islamic period.

The surface of the plateau at SBY 18 area was densely strewn with flint nodules and tiles on windblown sand and a grey beachrock base. There

Fig. 20. Ṣîr Banî Yâs: Site location SBY 18, 19, 23, 25.

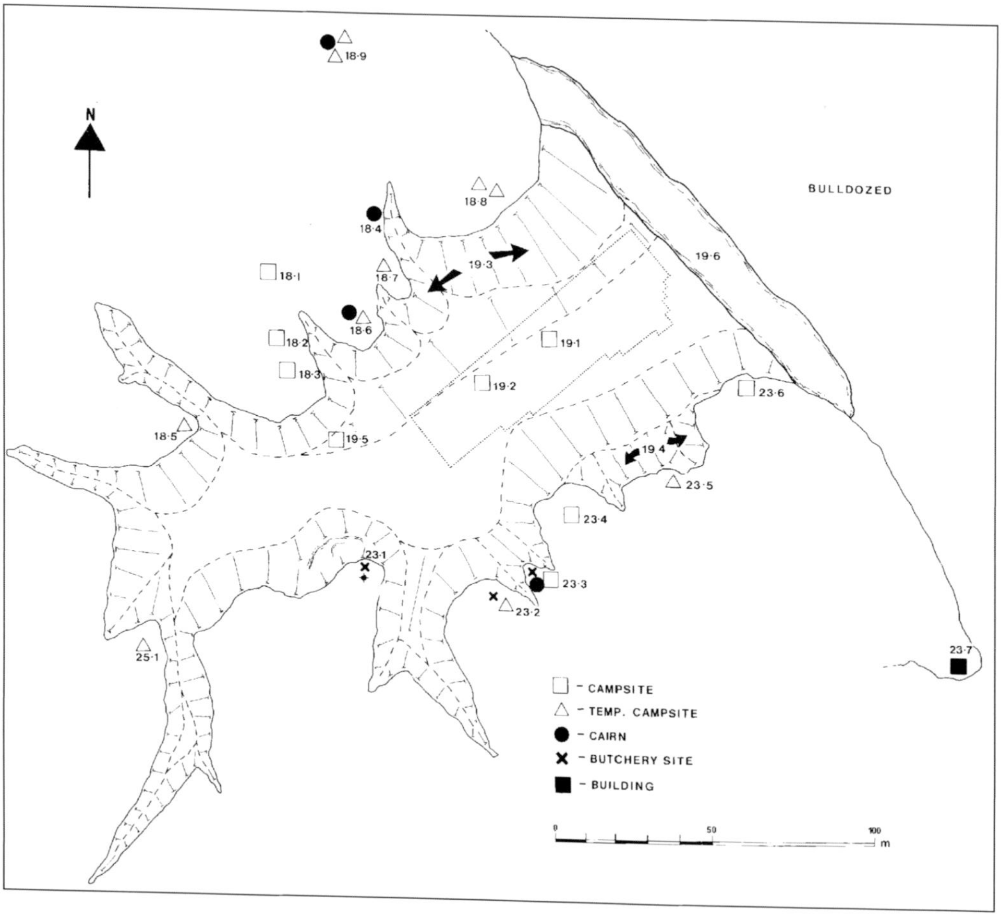

were occasional stray pieces of shell and modern glass, as well as ceramics and dugong bones. Tyre marks and other modern disturbance to the west led towards a dredgers' marker pole. The site was extremely fragile.

Date: 28.3.92 **Figs:** 4, 20. **Type:** Campsite **Period:** Late Islamic **SBY 18.1**

A sub-rectangular campsite, north of site SBY 18.2, with the natural flint surface cleaned back to make a space measuring a maximum of 11.5 m. x 7 m. There were the remains of a stone fireplace to the west, and weight stones to the east. Three clear sections suggested living space, presumably of an *ʿarîsh* with a possible entrance opening in the west side. It had a series of discrete elements, some or all of which may have been inter-related. It is assumed that reed-huts – *ʿarîsh* – rather than tents are indicated by these traces: this is assumed throughout this report at all camping sites.

Date: 28.3.92 **Figs:** 4, 20. **Type:** Campsite **Period:** Late Islamic **SBY 18.2**

This was a small cleared sub-square encampment south of SBY 18.1. It measured 5.5 m^2. with the remains of a small fireplace to the west and several stones to east and centre which possibly served as weights for a temporary structure. There were no finds.

Date: 28.3.92 **Figs:** 4, 20. **Type:** Campsite **Period:** Late Islamic **SBY 18.3**

This was a small cleared encampment south of SBY 18.2, directly above site SBY 19.5. It was a small cleared sub-square with a possible path on the south side but no other features. The main area measured 4.5 m^2. Eleven small depressions were noted in the plateau surface to the south of the encampment area.

Date: 28.3.92 **Figs:** 4, 20. **Type:** Cairn **Period:** Late Islamic **SBY 18.4**

This site was a small double cairn of flat flint tiles on a level, flint-strewn ridge, with a diameter of 1.00 - 1.5 m. and a maximum height of 20 cms.

Date: 28.3.92 **Figs:** 4, 20. **Type:** Depressions **Period:** Late Islamic **SBY 18.5**

An area of small depressions was formed by stone clearance of the ridge surface; some contained pot, glass and shell.

Date: 28.3.92 **Figs:** 4, 20. **Type:** Cairn **Period:** Late Islamic **SBY 18.6**

A group of four depressions, roughly circular, cleared of stones east of SBY 18.1, on a ridge to the north of site SBY 19, with diameters varying between 90 and 210 cms. Also a slight cairn of flint tiles (*ca* 10 cm), 80 cms in diameter.

SBY 18.7

Date: 28.3.92 **Figs:** 4, 20. **Type:** Depressions **Period:** Late Islamic

This was a group of seven small depressions on a flint strewn surface ranging between 60 cms and 1.2 m. in diameter. There were scatters of shell (mostly pearl), some pottery and also modern glass.

SBY 18.8

Date: 28.3.92 **Figs:** 4, 20. **Type:** Cairn (?) & depressions **Period:** Late Islamic

This was a possible small cairn of flint tiles, 80 cms in diameter, and a group of ten vague depressions in the ridge surface, 1 m. in diameter. Most of the depressions were very shallow. There were medium flint tiles, modern glass and pearl shell scattered across the ridge.

SBY 18.9

Date: 28.3.92 **Figs:** 4, 20. **Type:** Cairn **Period:** Late Islamic

Five depressions of cleared stones, mostly 1 m. deep.

Plate 14. Sites SBY 18, 19 and 23 near al-Ẓahir and Ra's Danân, Ṣîr Banî Yâs.

SBY 19

This was a later Islamic period campsite in a sandy gulley below the ridge on which sites SBY 18.1-18.9 were situated. It lay east of a mesa called Burqân Muhârij and near the shore, close to the south side of the dredgers' camp at Ra's Danân.

The gulley had been partly bulldozed to form a sand dyke at the east end. Like site SBY 18, it is described here as a series of discrete elements. No sherds or other artefacts were retrieved as it was intended to undertake a controlled pick-up of cultural remains at SBY 19 in the 1993 season.

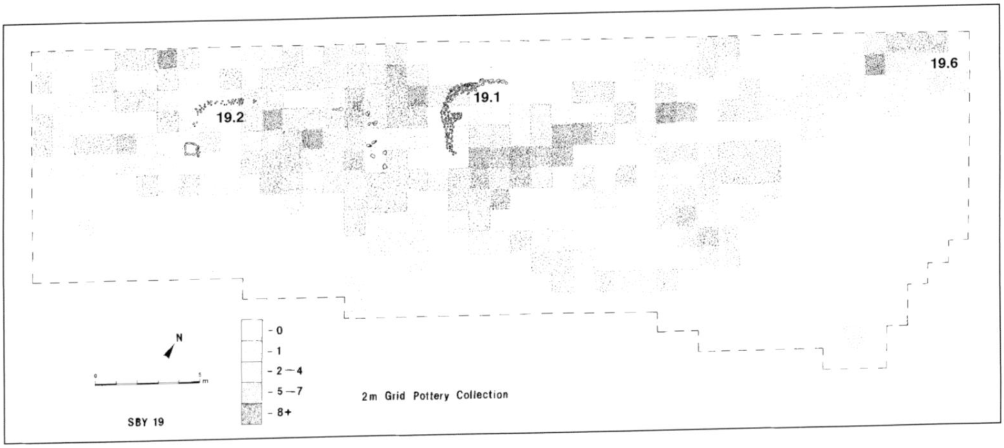

Fig. 21. *Ṣîr Banî Yâs: Site SBY 19. Ceramic distribution.*

SBY 19.1

Date: 28.3.92 **Figs:** 4, 20. **Type:** Structure **Period:** Late Islamic

This was the main area of an encampment where a temporary *ʿarîsh* rather than a tent was constructed in a sandy gulley below Site 19, probably in the Late Islamic period.

There was a raised, roughly crescent-shaped mound of stones and sand delineating a wall, 9.10 m. long and with a maximum height of *ca* 35 cms. It had an indented U-shaped feature to the west (a possible fireplace). The fireplace corners were built of larger shaped stones (35 cms x 11 cms x 30 cms). *Ca* 5 m. to the west were scatters of large stones, probably weights for walls. Another ridging with artefacts lay approximately 14 m. further east of the crescent wall which may mark the opposite side of the temporary structure. Finds included pottery and shell scatters.

Plate 15. Encampment (SBY 19.1), Ra's Danân, Ṣîr Banî Yâs.

Plate 16. Hearth near encampment SBY 19.1, Ṣîr Banî Yâs.

SBY 19.2

Date: 28.3.92 **Figs:** 4, 21. **Type:** Campsite **Period:** Late Islamic

Site SBY 19.2 was in the area to west of the crescent of SBY 19.1. Artefact scatters included large wall weights and shells, scattered over a total area of approximately 45 m. x 40 m. This scatter continued up the slope to the north to site SBY 19.3. There were two small groups of stones measuring 1.3 m. x 1.1 m. diameter. There was also a small rectangular stone structure, possibly a cistern in the gulley bed measuring 1.1 m. x 20 cms.

SBY 19.3

Date: 28.3.92 **Figs:** 4, 21. **Type:** Debris area **Period:** Late Islamic

This was a rich scatter of artefacts slipping down to SBY 19.1 and 19.2 and spread over the whole of the slope at the northern end of the wadi.

SBY 19.4

Date: 28.3.92 **Figs:** 4, 21. **Type:** Debris area **Period:** Late Islamic

At the east end of the gulley, on the southern slope, were scatters of artefacts.

SBY 19.5

Date: 28.3.92 **Figs:** 4. **Type:** Campsite **Period:**

This was a small encampment on the north side of the gulley in the central-west area, with groups of large-medium stones scattered over a cleared area: these were probably used as weights for an *ʿarîsh*. A roughly rectangular flat area measured approximately 5.70 m. x 5 m. The site had almost no artefacts, but sites SBY 18.1-18.3 stood immediately above on the plateau. SBY 19.6 was a sherd scatter at a bulldozed sand dam blocking the east end of the gulley.

Date: 26.3.92 **Figs:** 4, 14,16. **Type:** Cairn **Period:** Pre-Islamic (?) **SBY 20**

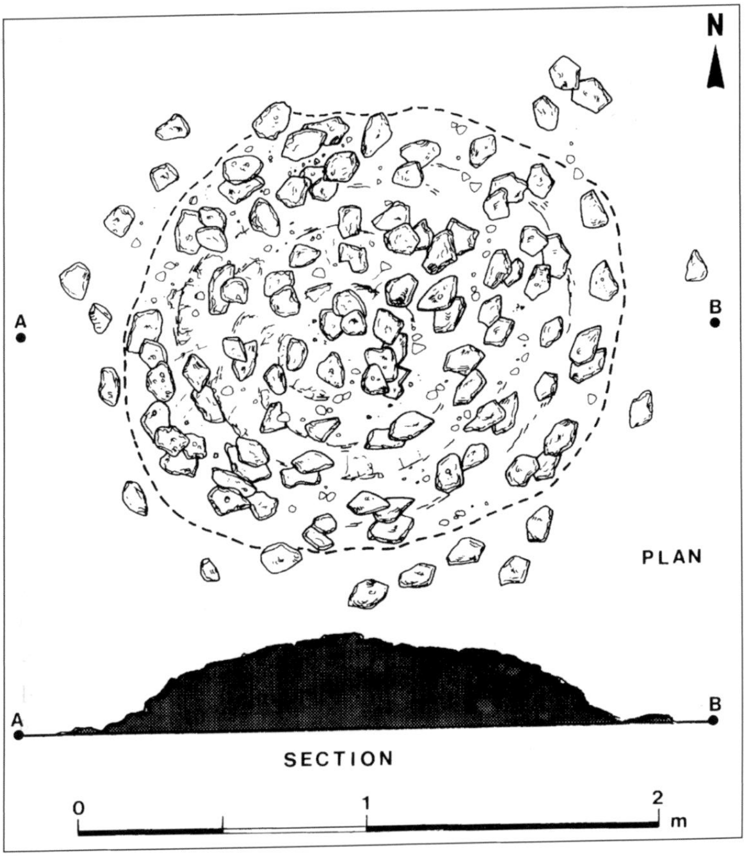

Fig. 22. Ṣîr Banî Yâs: Site SBY 20.

This was a small circular cairn about 1 m. NW of a prominent white dovecot on an eminence near al-Nakhayl. It was 2.30 m. in diameter and it stood about 60 cms high. The cairn was mostly of flint construction, with flints *ca* 10 cms x 8 cms x 3 cms. There were two further concentrations of stone, one 4.5 m. north and the other 4 m. east of the main standing cairn, suggesting the remains of other cairns. None of the sherds retrieved were found on the cairn.

AL-ẒAHIR (Fig. 4)

The name al-Ẓahir (or al-Thahir) attaches itself to a series of separate settlement sites, all abandoned and ruined amidst the plantation enclosures on the northern side of the island. Al-Ẓahir and ʿAwâfî, a second village on the west side of Ṣîr Banî Yâs, were abandoned by their populations earlier this century when the people moved to Dalmâ. The remains of al-Ẓahir were near the old beach and also inland. They were so disturbed by the plantations that it is no longer possible to plot or measure the scanty remains.

SBY 21

Date: 27.3.92 **Figs:** 4. **Type:** Settlement **Period:** Late Islamic

Site SBY 21 (and site SBY 14) was a part of the abandoned village of al-Ẓahir, lying 0.7 km SSE and inland from the distinctive dovecot beside site SBY 20. The traces of the walls of a 9 m. x 2.5 m. rectangular stone structure with an internal dividing wall were identified. This building lay to the south side of the track. There were also other foundation traces up-slope in the vicinity.

Within the neighbouring plantation enclosure to the north and NW there were once said to have been structures, but these had vanished and all that marked their presence were occasional groupings of beach rock.

SBY 22

Date: 27.3.92 **Figs:** 4. **Type:** Well & house remains **Period:** Late Islamic

Site SBY 22 was the area of al-Ẓahir nearer to the coast, within a modern fenced plantation. Beach stone heaps lay within the plantation enclosure to the north and east.

A blocked well was pointed out to us at the northern end of the coastal village. It was *ca* 3.8 m. in diameter, with only the northern steyning visible. There were also areas of stony rubble to the east and west. The graveyard site SBY 11.2 was related to the coastal al-Ẓahir, lying immediately to its south. The camp sites in the gulley to the north (Site SBY 19) and on the plateau above (Site SBY 18) all seemed to be related to the SBY 22 village site.

SBY 23

Site SBY 23 lay on the ridge south of Site SBY 19. In much the same manner as Site SBY 18 and Site SBY 19, it comprised numerous individual elements which were part of a larger unit. Many if not all of these elements at Site SBY 23 were datable to a long period of time, and were related to hunting and food preparation activities. However, an emphatically early element was only noted at Site 23.4, indicated by lithic artefacts.

SBY 23.1

Date: 28.3.92 **Figs:** 4, 20. **Type:** Butchery site **Period:** Late Islamic (?)

Site SBY 23.1 was at the central NW end of the plateau, west of Sites SBY 18 and 19: it was a scatter of artefacts over the surface measuring 10 m^2. on top of the ridge. The presence of dugong bone indicated a (recent?) butchering site.

SBY 23.2

Date: 28.3.92 **Figs:** 4, 20. **Type:** Butchery site **Period:** Late Islamic

Site SBY 23.2 was at the central NW end of the southern plateau near Ra's Danân and consisted of scuffed surface areas and depressions. The eastern depression was deeper (diameter: 1 m.; depth: 20 cms) with a heaped soil cairn to the SW. About 30 dugong bones (ribs, vertebrae etc.) were found in an area 20 m. x 10 m. overlooking site SBY 19.

Date: 28.3.92 **Figs:** 4, 20. **Type:** Campsite, butchery site **Period:** Late Islamic **SBY 23.3**

This was a small rectangular cleared area (4.4 m. x 2.6 m.) with a low stone and soil mound (diameter 1.30 cms). Artefacts included late glass, pearl shells and dugong bones.

Date: **Figs:** 4, 20. **Type:** Campsite **Period:** Late Islamic (?)/Late Stone Age (?) **SBY 23.4**

This was a cleared area measuring 7 m. x 4.5 m. outlined by heaped stones, with two compartments (N area 3 m. x 2.5 m.; S area 2.5 m. x 1.5 m.): it is assumed to have been an *ʿarîsh* structure rather than a tent. Finds included a tile knife, pottery and shells. A possible hearth 90 cms x 70 cms was located 3 m. to the east.

Date: 28.3.92 **Figs:** 4, 20. **Type:** Pottery scatter **Period:** Late Islamic **SBY 23.5**

This was a pottery scatter, 5 m^2., including Julfâr ware at the NE end of the ridge.

Date: 28.3.92 **Figs:** 4, 20. **Type:** Campsite **Period:** Late Islamic **SBY 23.6**

Two rectangular cleared spaces (3.7 m. x 2.4 m. and 2.1 m. x 2.4 m.) with activity areas to east and SE. There was a small soil and stone mound to the NE and two depressions to the SE. Finds noted included Far Eastern porcelain, retouched flints, modern glass, and shells.

Date: **Figs:** 4, 20. **Type:** Structure **Period:** Late Islamic **SBY 23.7**

A sub-square structure situated on the ridge above wadis to the east and south, behind al-Ẓahir village (site SBY 22). There were beach rock structural remains approximately 10 m^2. and about 1.5-2 m. high with no obvious mortar. Finds noted included small flints, Julfâr-type pottery, late glass, and pearl shells. Modern iron shrapnel was also found, presumably from the post-1966 period when the island was used for target practice by British and Emirates forces.

SBY 24

Site SBY 24 was situated on two low elongated ridges to the SW of the Ra's Danân dredgers' camp and 250 m. SW of Site SBY 19 gulley. It lay on the plateau behind the coastal ridge and just north of the asphalt road that ran around the perimeter of the island.

Ridges of grey crystalline beach rock were divided by a shallow gulley that ran down to the west. The ridge surfaces were covered with medium flint gravel and aeolian sand. The largest flints were on the ridge and the slope and included flint tiles and nodules along with occasional grey, more calcareous stones. The tile flint was generally dark brown, sometimes with black desert polish. Several pieces of worked flint were recovered. There was no evidence of debitage but washing out of the deflated surface may have caused this loss.

SBY 24.1

Date: 28.3.92 **Figs:** 4. **Type:** Cairns & worked flint **Period:** Late Stone Age (?)

Site SBY 24.1 covered an area 80 m. x 70 m. on the long ridge standing about 2 m. above the plateau. A scatter of worked flints was located on the top of the ridge. On the ridge top were three to four small possible cairns (SBY 24.3, 24.4 and 24.5).

SBY 24.2

Date: 28.3.92 **Figs:** 4. **Type:** Worked flint **Period:** Late Stone Age (?)

Site SBY 24.2 lay NW of site SBY 24.1 and was 200-250 m. SW of Site 19. It was on the irregular eastern part of the N/S running ridge, approximately 100 m. x 45 m. in area, with several features (Sites SBY 24.6, 24.7, 24.8). Worked flint was noted. The east side of the site was disturbed by car-tracks.

SBY 24.3

Date: 28.3.92 **Figs:** 4. **Type:** Cairn(s) **Period:** Pre-Islamic (?)

Site SBY 24.3 was in the centre north area of the ridge where site SBY 24.1 was located: it was NW of SBY 24.4 and NE of SBY 25.5. It was a low stone cairn (diameter 1.6 m. and 20 cms high) of brown grey flints. There was a second possible cairn immediately to the north, approximately 1 m. in diameter.

SBY 24.4

Date: 28.3.92 **Figs:** 4. **Type:** Cairn **Period:** Pre-Islamic (?)

Site SBY 24.4 was a deflated small stone cairn of brown and grey flints (diameter 2.4 m.-2.3 m. and maximum 20-30 cms high) in the centre of ridge SBY 24.1; it was 12 m. SE of SBY 24.3 and east of SBY 24.5.

SBY 24.5

Date: 28.3.92 **Figs:** 4. **Type:** Cairn **Period:** Pre-Islamic (?)

Site SBY 24.5 was in the centre west of site SBY 24.1, lying 17 m. SW of site SBY 24.3 and 17 m. NW of site SBY 24.4. It was a small stone cairn, badly deflated and ruinous. Its maximum diameter was 85 cms and its maximum height was 10-20 cms. On the top of the ridge on which site SBY 24.1 was located there were stone outlines – some of which were rectilinear. These were either structures, a working area or graves.

Date: 28.3.92 **Figs:** 4. **Type:** Curved stone feature **Period:** ?

SBY 24.6

Site SBY 24.6 was on the NE slope of ridge 24.2, and 5 m. from the western edge of the wadi beneath; it continued to the extreme northern edge of the ridge. It was a curved, linear stone feature formed of a single course, level with the surface: it was at least 10 m. and possibly 30 m. long. It was of dry-stone construction using flints 10 cm^2. with a possible break along its length. It may have been an encampment border enclosing the upper part of the ridge or the remains of a structure.

Date: 28.3.92 **Figs:** 4. **Type:** Cairns? **Period:** ?

SBY 24.7

Site SBY 24.7 was on the lower east slope of ridge SBY 24.2, roughly 30 m. NW of the southern edge of the ridge. It was NW of site SBY 24.8. It was an area of possible stone cairns or burials, covering 15 m^2. It may have been a natural feature.

Date: 28.3.92 **Figs:** 4. **Type:** Cairn **Period:** ?

SBY 24.8

Site SBY 24.8 was situated 12 m. north of the southern end of ridge SBY 24.2, and 15 m. east of the wadi edge. It was a possible small stone cairn measuring 1.20 m. in diameter with a maximum height of 20 cms, made of flints measuring *ca* 10 cm^2.

Date: 28.3.92 **Figs:** 4. **Type:** Depression **Period:** ?

SBY 25

Site SBY 25 was west of site SBY 19, on the plateau overlooking the gulley. It was a shallow depression cleared of stones: it was 80 cms in diameter and 2 cms deep.

Date: 29.3.92 **Figs:** 4. **Type:** Graves **Period:** Late Islamic (?)

SBY 26

Site SBY 26 was *ca* 50 m. NE of site SBY 24.1, north of the asphalt road. It consisted of a group of at least seven late Islamic graves (SBY 26.1-26.7). They were marked out by flat tile flints; most lacked a headstone.

Date: 28.3.92 **Figs:** 4. **Type:** Cairns **Period:** Pre-Islamic (?)

SBY 27

Site SBY 27 was situated on the extreme SE ridge of a flint strewn sandy plateau area lying to the west of a wadi which in turn lay immediately west of ridge SBY 24.1: it was north of the tarmac road. It consisted of two cairns. Iron shrapnel was found on this plateau.

Sites SBY 28 to 30

The results of the survey of the north-west and west of the island were extremely meagre in terms of site identification compared with those from the east and the north. The coastal plain here had been heavily planted and disturbed while the higher ridges behind the NW coastal plain produced only meagre results (sites SBY 28-30 and 36).

On the western coast there was formerly the late Islamic period village of ᶜAwâfî. Its site is now inside the plantations, immediately east of the landing strip. There was some beach rock among the bulldoze at the margins of the plantations which seemed to be the remains of the ᶜAwâfî houses, but nothing else remained. Sites SBY 32-34 were almost certainly related to ᶜAwâfî and presumably were contemporaneous with it.

SBY 28

Date: 29.3.92 **Figs:** 4. **Type:** Cairn **Period:** Pre-Islamic (?)

Site 28 was on the north edge of a high ridge on the western side of the island, lying to the east of the plantations. It was an oval cairn of small-medium multicoloured stones with maximum dimensions of 1.10 m. x 0.80 m. x 0.30 m.

SBY 29

Date: 29.3.92 **Figs:** 4. **Type:** Cairn **Period:** Pre-Islamic (?)

The site was on the NW edge of a high bluff in the foothills on the west side of the island. It was a sub-oval/rectangular cairn, 1.5 m. x 2 m. x 0.3 m. high, with multi-coloured, medium sized stones. It was partly destroyed.

SBY 30

This site was in the NW of the island, to the east of the plantations of Qarn Bû ᶜAlma. It lay *ca* 50 m. NW of the tarmac road around the island, and below a ridge on a sandy plain. It had two main elements, Sites SBY 30.1 and 30.3.

SBY 30.1

Date: 29.3.92 **Figs:** 4. **Type:** Campsite **Period:** Late Islamic

Site SBY 30.1 was a campsite in a sub-circular cleared space measuring *ca* 8 m. x 4 m. with stone weights.

SBY 30.2

Date: 29.3.92 **Figs:** 4. **Type:** Cairn **Period:** Pre-Islamic (?)

Site SBY 30.2 lay at the NW corner of a small hillock *ca* 150 m. NW of the road and east of the Qarn Bû ᶜAlma plantations. It was a small sub-circular cairn *ca* 2 m. x 1.5 m. and stood only 15-20 cms high. Its orientation was to 300° which suggested that it was pre-Islamic.

Date: 29.3.92 **Figs:** 4. **Type:** Graves **Period:** Islamic

SBY 30.3

Site SBY 30.3 was *ca* 10 m. north of the tarmac road, to the east of the Qarn Bû ʿAlma plantations. There were two, possibly three, Islamic burials. There may have been more burials obscured by sand.

Date: 27.3.92 **Figs:** 4. **Type:** Cairns **Period:** Pre-Islamic (?)

SBY 31

Site SBY 31 was on the ridge overlooking the llama pens at Khawr al-Janûbî to the NW of Site 16. There was a row of three small stone cairns (SBY 31.1, 31.2 and 31.3) lying near each other and running along a north-south axis. They were sub-circular groups of stone (maximum diameter, 2 m.) built with flat flint tiles, 10 m^2. They were slightly raised in the centre to a maximum of 10 cms. There were no finds.

Date: 29.3.92 **Figs:** 4. **Type:** Encampment & fishing/pearling beach **Period:** Late Islamic

SBY 32

This was a site on a sandy beach on the west side of the island. It was 32 m. west of the tarmac road and opposite the gate to the Oryal enclosure: it was south of site SBY 33 to which it was related. There were several rectangular features on the stone strewn sandy beach. SBY 32.1 was a rectangular group of loose stones measuring 1.5 m. x 1 m.: SBY 32.2 measuring 2 m. x 1 m. was of the same character. The artefact scatters were like those on beach site SBY 33 in terms of ceramics.

Date: 29.3.92 **Figs:** 4. **Type:** Campsite **Period:** Late Islamic

SBY 33

This was a beach on the west side of the island in the area of Mufalaja, 2.6 kms from the north end of the airstrip and just south of al-Bâb. It

Plate 17. Beach campsite (SBY 33) at Mufalaja on the west side of Ṣîr Banî Yâs.

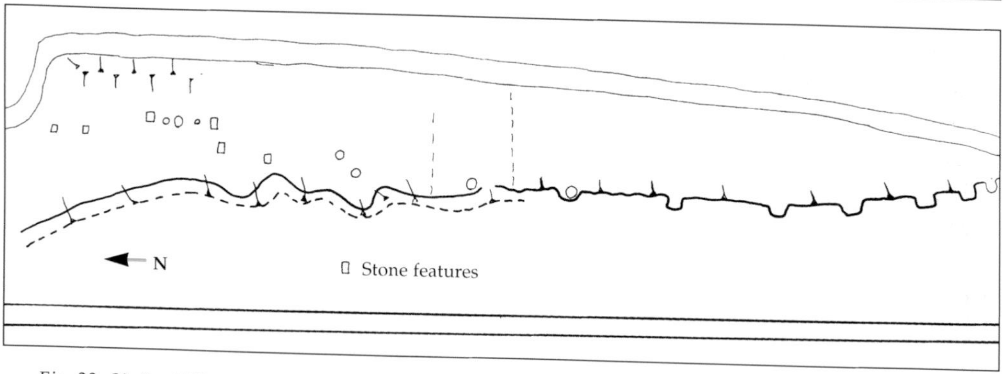

Fig. 23. Ṣîr Banî Yâs: Site SBY 33. Pearling beach, Mufalaja.

was used in the past as a pearling camp. The occupation area was about 1100 m. x 120 m. and reached as far as the high water mark.

There was a small jutting promontory at the south end of the beach with a shell midden measuring 180 m. x 40 m. and 3 m. high: it consisted of 90% pearl shells. The beach to the north and east had a continuous scatter of shell and occasional dugong bones, along with other small middens to the east of the main southern midden. There were rectangular and circular stone features.

The entire length of the beach was scattered with artefacts, including glazed and unglazed ceramics, Chinese celadon, glass and shell. There were several flattened dumps of modern plantation debris (rubber tubing, bamboo, twigs and hessian). Mr al-Ghossain told us that pearling had continued on this beach until recent years. However, the ceramic horizon indicated that it had been in use over several centuries during the Late Islamic period.

SBY 34

Date: 29.3.92 **Figs:** 4. **Type:** Cemetery **Period:** Late Islamic

The site was situated in a flat dune area just above the present beach on the west side of the island. It was 1.9 km north of the airport and 98 m. west of the tarmac road. There were four Islamic period burials and a triangular stone cairn in an area 10 m. x 8 m. The graves were all of the same character. There was a large, thick double stone at the head and foot of each grave, and mounded sandy soil and small white pebbles. These burials probably were related to sites SBY 32 and 33 to the north and/or to ʿAwâfî village.

SBY 35

Date: 29.3.92 **Figs:** 4. **Type:** Tower **Period:** Late Islamic ?

The site of a destroyed tower lay on the west side of the tarmac road on the east side of Ṣîr Banî Yâs, towards the north end of Khawr al-Janûbî. Although the tower had vanished, the remains of scattered masonry, perhaps of its stone base, was noted in the vicinity. From local accounts, it appeared to have had stone lower courses and clay construction in the superstructure. Such towers have been discussed at length by D. Kennet[21].

To the NW, inside the plantation where there were tall, old established trees, there was a natural depression which filled with water after rain. People on Dalmâ who knew Ṣîr Banî Yâs described the tower as being intended to guard the water. They said that the tower had a stone base and clay superstructure, with hooded firing points of a character still extant elsewhere in the UAE.

Date: 30.3.92 **Figs:** 4, 24. **Type:** Mine **Period:** ? **SBY 36**

On the west side of the mountains in the centre of the island in an area called Wadi'l-Milḥ was a salt mine. Wadi'l-Milḥ itself ran down to the west side of the island. Six mine entrances were visible, including deep shafts. The mine was inaccessible because of debris and infilling and it had become dangerous. Subsidence was visible over the entire area, suggesting underground tunnelling. In three places, salt was exposed in the rock face, being used as licks by the gazelles which were numerous here. Mr al-Ghossain said that 20 years earlier (*ca* 1972), tools were found in one of the shafts at the end of the gulley leading to the mine.

Plate 18. Salt mine at Wâdî'l-Milḥ (SBY 36), Ṣîr Banî Yâs.

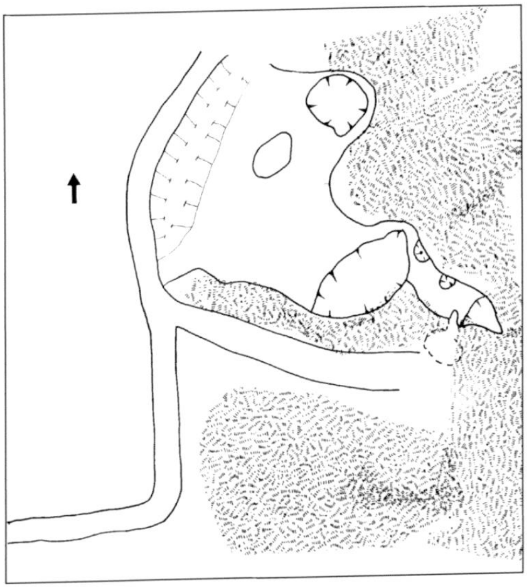

Fig. 24. Salt-mine: Site SBY 32.

Notes

1 Compared with the other islands surveyed, mapping for Ṣîr Banî Yâs is good. See for example, "Approaches to J. az Zannah & Ar Ru'ays", Ser. K. 867, ed. 2-GSGS, 1:25,000.
"Admiralty Chart, published Taunton, 8.7.77, ed. 1980, 1:35,000.
Series 1501, Sheet NG 39-15, Edition 7-GSGS, 1:250,000 Umm Sa'id (Musay'id), Qatar; United Arab Emirates, Saudi Arabia (1992).

2 See Series 1501, Sheet NG 39-15, Edition 7-GSGS, 1:250,000.

3 B.J. Slot, *The Arabs of the Gulf, 1602-1784. An alternative approach to the early history of the Arab Gulf States and the Arab peoples of the Gulf, mainly based on sources of the Dutch East India Company*, Leidschenden (1993), p. 38.

4 Captain Robert Taylor, "The Persian Gulf" in "Extracts from brief notes, containing historical and other information connected with the province of Oman; Muskat and the adjoining country; the islands of Bahrein, Ormus, Kishm, and Karrack; and other ports and places in the Persian Gulf", Bombay (1818), in *Selection from the records of the Bombay Government*, no. xxix, New Series, Bombay (1856), pp. 16-17.

5 India Office Records , P/385/33 *Bombay Political Proceedings, Bombay Gazette* (26th March, 1823), p. 2533. See also C. C. Mann, *Abu Dhabi: Birth of an Oil Shaikhdom*, Beirut (1969), p. 26.

6 "Seer Bani Yas, distant 6 miles---From a sketch by Dr Maskell [IOR x/40310/17], in *Survey of the Shores and Islands of the Persian Gulf, 1820-1829*, vol. 5, Map 49.
Trigonometrical Survey of the Arabian or Southern Side of the Persian Gulf, by Lieuts. J.M. Guy + G.B. Brucks, H.C. Marine 1824, Sheet 2nd (from Abu Dhabi to Sir Bani Yas) Published 1st September 1826 [IOR: x/3630/20/21], in *Survey of the Shores and Islands of the Persian Gulf, 1820-1829*, vol. 2, Map 8.
Trigonometrical Survey of the Shores off the Entrance to Abuthubbee Backwater on the Arabian side of the Persian Gulf, by Lieuts. J.M. Guy + G.B. Brucks, H.C. Marine 1823. Drawn by Lieut. M. Houghton, H.C.M. [IOR: x/3691], in *Survey of the Shores and Islands of the Persian Gulf, 1820-1829*, vol. 4, Map 27.
Plan of the Island + Harbour of Beni Yas, by Lieuts. G.B. Brucks + R. Logan, 1822 [IOR: x/3692].

7 John Tallis and Co., *Arabia*, London and New York (*ca* 1823).

8 J.S. Buckingham, *Travel in Assyria, Media and Persia*, London (1829), pp. 450-451.

9 Although today channels leading out of the ports of Jabal Dhanna and Ra's al-Mughayraq opposite Ṣîr Banî Yâs have been dredged, much of the water between Ṣîr Banî Yâs and the mainland is very shallow and only navigable by small boats. Reefs break surface at low tide, and the water level in many places drops to less than a fathom.

10 Captain George Barnes Brucks, "Memoir descriptive of the Navigation of the Gulf of Persia, with brief notes of the Manners, Customs, Religions, Commerce and Resources of the People inhabiting its shore and islands, in *Selection from the Records of the Bombay Government*, no. xxix, New Series, Bombay (1856), p. 553.

11 J. Hansburgh, ed. A.A. Taylor, *The India Directory*, London (1891), Section III, pp. 245-6.

12 J.G. Lorimer, *Gazetteer of the Persian Gulf, 'Omân, and Central Arabia*, Calcutta (1908), IIB, pp. 1931-2.

13 *Persian Gulf Pilot comprising the Persian Gulf and its approaches, from Ras al Hadd, in the south-west, to Cape Monze, in the East*, 8th ed., London (1932), p. 181; pp. 184-5.

14 D. Lee, *Flight from the Middle East. A history of the Royal Air Force in the Arabian Peninsula and adjacent territories 1945-1972*, London (1980), p. 267.

15 Vogt, *et al.*, *op. cit.*, p. 50.

16 C. Lehmann, "Pottery Sherds, Ṣîr Bani Yas, 2-3 May, 1991", unpublished report.

17 Communication, 1.3.1992.

18 The team arrived at Ṣîr Banî Yâs by UAE military aircraft from Abu Dhabi on 24th March, 1992 and in the afternoon were taken on an initial circumambulation of the island by Dr Najih,who is responsible for tourism and acts as veterinary surgeon on the island. We visited the archaeological areas known to Dr Najih and Mr Ghassan al-Ghossain and those which had been seen by Mrs Lehmann, to give us some idea of the nature of the area.

19 See DA 2, p. 50 below.

20 Site 17, on further examination, proved to be of no archaeological significance.

21 D. Kennet, *The Towers of Ras al-Khaimah*, Oxford (1995), *passim*.

DALMÂ (DA)

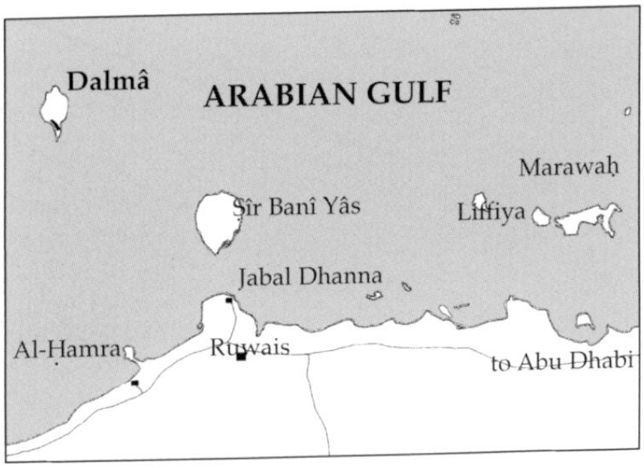

Dalmâ (Delma) is an island at UTM 6333000° E/2710000° N, lying 29.5 kms from Şîr Banî Yâs and 80 kms from the eastern coast of Qaṭar. It measures 9 kms from north to south and 5 kms from east to west, rising to 98 m. It is volcanic and mountainous with most of the rocky terrain quite barren. Immediately to the south was once a smaller island, now attached to the main island by a modern landfill peninsula. The main settlement, also called Dalmâ, is at the southern tip of the island. The island has a population today of some 6000-7000 people. In the past it is remembered locally to have had a permanent population which was made possible by the presence of wells near the town of Dalmâ, in the area where there are now newly established farms. Brucks in 1829 said that water was brackish at Dalmâ and Lorimer in 1908 reported that it was plentiful but brackish. We were told that formerly the island had 200 wells, some sweet, others more saline. The water in the only well still visible in the farms was sweet. The local people report that water was formerly sent from Dalmâ to other places including Abu Dhabi, because of its good quality: this was still happening as recently as the early 1950s. This transport of water around the Gulf seems to have been common. Less than two generations ago, water was brought from al-Başra to Kuwait[1] and it seems to have been a widespread practice in the area.

There are few references to Dalmâ in the past. The Venetian jeweller Gasparo Balbi in 1590, mentioned "Delmephialmas" in his list of places amidst the pearl beds but he gave no details of it[2].

Captain Maude in the early 1820s recorded Dalmâ as follows[3]:

> *Delamee is in lat. 24° 36′ north, and long. 52° 24′ east. Its length from north to south is about six miles, and its breadth less than half that, from east to west. It is of moderate height, and of a darker colour than Arzeneeah* [to the east]. *On its northern end, is a round hill, the extremity of which terminates in a low sand; and towards the southern point there are three small hummocks, which slope off in a similar way. Off the northern end of the island, a shoal extends for nearly two miles in that direction, which ought not to be approached under seven fathoms; and the passage to the southward of the island, or between it and the Arabian shore, is considered as altogether unsafe. The channel between Delamee and Arzeneeah is, however, clear of shoals; though there are in it irregular soundings and overfalls, from twenty-one to fifteen, and from twelve to seven fathoms.*

Captain Brucks in 1829 recorded Dalmâ in the following terms[4]:

ISLAND OF DALMY
The south point of the island of Dalmy is in lat. 24° 27′ 35″ N., and long. 52° 27′ 25″ E. The island is rather high, and in the centre is a remarkably flat hill. Its south point is low, and has some wells of brackish water in it. Two miles below the south point is situated Arlaat Mussooma, a small sandy island. There is no danger off Dalmy, except between the south point and the sandy island, which you may round a mile distant to the southward, in seven fathoms. This island, like most others about this part, seems of volcanic origin. It is the next largest to Seer Beniyas of what are generally called Mandes Islands.

According to *The India Directory* of 1891, Dalmâ was the only island on the Pearl Banks that had a permanent population. The island is described as follows[5]:

Dalmah, or Delmy, the S. end, in lat., 24° 27½′ N., lon. 52° 19½′ E., lying 20 m. to the S.W. of Arzanah, is 244 ft. high, of darker colour than ... [Arzanah], and about 5 m. long from N. to S., and 2½ m. broad. On its n. part is a round hill, below which the boundary is bluff, but not high; and excepting at the S. point, the island may be approached to 7 fathoms. To the S.E. it is nearly of equal height, with two or three hummocks above a very low, narrow, sandy point, which extends from N. to S., terminating the S. extremity; beyond which a shoal spit of 1 fathom extends a dry sand-bank, Kalat Masuma, at 3 m. distance. There is no safe passage for large vessels to the S. of this island, on account of sudden overfalls. The sea between it and the Goodwin Islands (Kaffay and Mayamat-et-tein), has not been sounded, but extensive shoals lie more than 12 m. to E. of the latter. The channel between Dalmah and Arzanah is clear of shoals, but the overfalls are sudden, from 8 to 20 fathoms, fine coral sand.

According to Lorimer, Dalmâ was a centre for the pearl trade, with pearl banks to the north, the north-west, the south-west and to the south-east. A revenue of $5000 (*i.e.* Maria Theresa dollars) was derived annually from the taxation on Dalmâ's pearl trade[6]. The local inhabitants dived in summer and gathered pearls by wading out to the pearl-banks in winter. At the time that Lorimer wrote (1908) there were some 15 families of the Qubaisât section of the Banî Yâs living at the small settlement on the southern coastal plain towards its western end[7]. In the early years of this century, according to Lorimer, a temporary bazaar would be set up at Dalmâ at the end of each pearling season. Accounts would be settled among pearl traders at this market, and Lorimer specifically mentions Indian merchants of the Trucial Omani coast visiting the Dalmâ bazaar, buying pearls and receiving settlement of debts[8]. We were told that the island was locally called Bombay in the past, so large were the numbers of Indian merchants who would come there to trade in pearls.

Plate 19. *The mountains in the centre of Dalmâ island.*

The *Persian Gulf Pilot* of 1932 describes Dalmâ and the waters offshore[9], repeating Lorimer's observations. A single village (*i.e.* Dalmâ) is mentioned on the western side of the plain at the southern end of the island; it was small and had a tower which could be seen from the sea from eastward. There was plenty of water but it was brackish. The people of the island kept herds of goats. The anchorage for local boats was on the western side of the southern point of the island, off the village. This seems to have been near the al-Muraykhî Pearl House. It is also recorded that Dalmâ "... is much visited by the pearl boats on account of the water, and at the end of the season a temporary bazaar is set up; persons engaged in the trade, including the Indian merchants of the Trucial coast, go there to collect debts and purchase pearls".

We were able to glean information about the island's past from the local people. It had been very populous until some two centuries ago when smallpox struck. Outbreaks of the disease wiped out much of the population, leaving no more than 15 people according to one account. These left and went elsewhere. The smallpox was confined to Dalmâ by closing other ports to boats from the island. Before the smallpox outbreak, Dalmâ had been a major commercial centre in the area.

Several archaeologists have visited Dalmâ according to B. Vogt[10], who records visits to Dalmâ and the Jabal Dhanna area on the mainland by Geoffrey Bibby, Serge Cleuziou, Karen Frifelt and Walid al-Tikriti. An Iraqi mission undertook limited excavations in 1975 at an Islamic site on Dalmâ but no report has ever been published: we were shown the location of the excavated site, but it had been entirely bulldozed.

S. Cleuziou has summarized the archaeological sites noted by a French expedition of September-October, 1979, but no other report seems to be available[11]. So little is recorded of Dalmâ, and so much has changed since 1979, that Cleuziou's comments are particularly valuable as a record of what remained at that time:

> *Comme partout, l'irruption de la vie est à Dalmâ une menace pour les vestiges du passé. Il reste actuellement trois sites archéologiques certains. Deux d'entre eux, sur la côte, sont d'époque islamique recente (18-19 siècle), le troisième, entre le village actuel et les collines est attribuable à l'époque sassanide ou au tout debut de l'Islam (400-800 après J.C.). C'est là une periode mal connue qu'il serait du plus haut interêt d'étudier à Dalmâ. Trois mosquées et une habitation ancienne typiques de la construction traditionnelle du Golfe meritent d'être restaurées. Parmi de très nombreux tumulus naturels quelques-uns sont très probablement artificiels et devront être fouillés...*
> *Fouilles archéologiques*
> *Au nord de la palmerai, un fort (?) et une maison datant du debut de l'Islam (ou de l'époque sassanide) devraient être fouillés en premier tandis que serait delimitée l'etendue exacte du site entier*[12].
> *Certains tumuli devraient être sondés, pour verifier s'il s'agit bien de tombes qui'il faudrait alors fouiller.*
> *De nombreux sites possibles doivent être verifiés.*

Cleuziou's archaeological map is instructive, reflecting the degree of loss in the intervening 20 years. We saw the remaining sites in more degraded condition, justifying the anxieties that he expressed about the threat posed by development.

It has been suggested that a Nestorian Christian diocese was based at Dalmâ in the Sassanian period, although it has also been argued that the diocese was located at Samahîj on the Bahraini island of al-Muḥarraq[13].

The range of finds at the Dalmâ sites reflects the long history of the island. The discovery of ʿUbaid pottery at DA 11/DA 12.1 demonstrates that there was human activity at Dalmâ in the 4th or 5th millennium BC, and this is one of the most important discoveries of the survey. There is also evidence of Sassanian-Early Islamic pottery from DA 7.1 and 7.3 which shows settlement on the island in the 1st millennium AD, while middle and later Islamic pottery is represented, indicating settlement into late periods. It is interesting to note the presence of imported Chinese pottery including celadon which is of the same *ca* 14th century date that we find at other coastal sites in the region, especially at Julfâr in Ra's al-Khaimah.

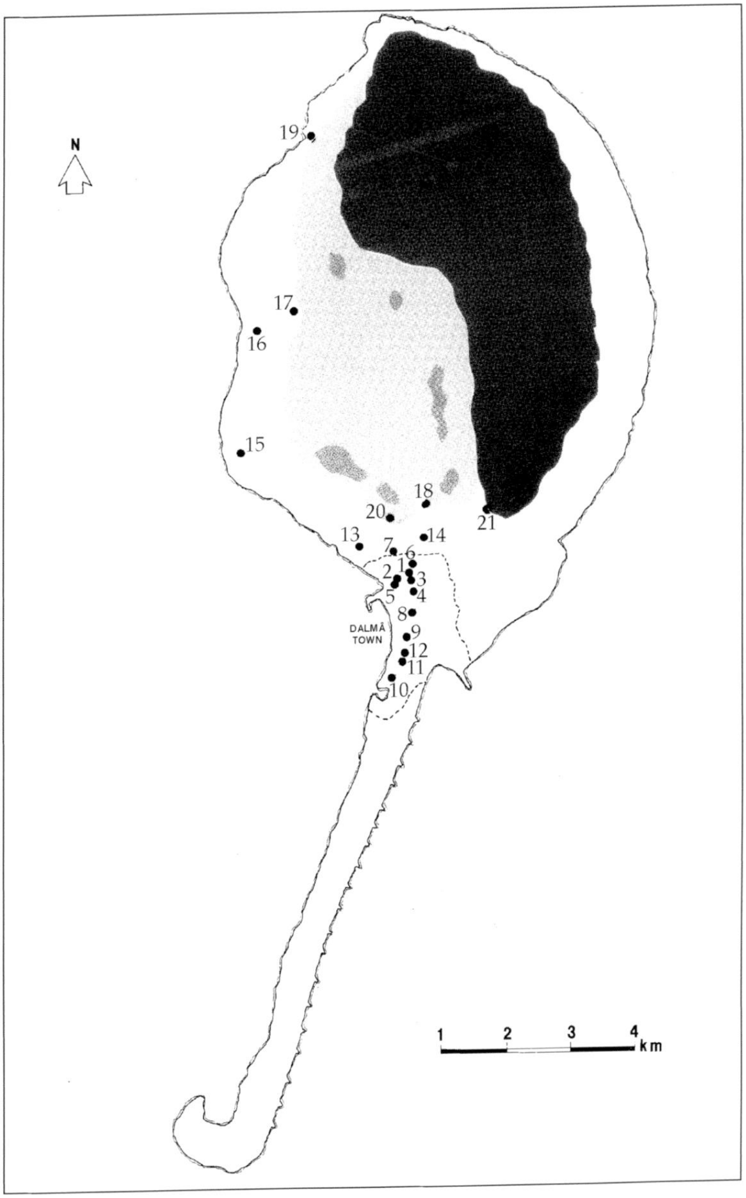

Fig. 25. Dalmâ: Site locations.

THE SITES

Date: 1.4.92 **Figs:** 25. **Type:** Mosque **Period:** Late Islamic **DA 1**

The mosque of Muḥammad b. Jâsim al-Muraykhî was situated *ca* 100 m. north of the National Bank of Abu Dhabi in Dalmâ town. It was associated with the Muraykhî Pearling House (DA 2). The mosque measured 14.2 m. N/S and 17.2 E/W overall and consisted of a prayer hall on the *qibla* side and an open court on the east side. The only feature in the courtyard was a low square prayer platform measuring 1 m. a side

Plate 20 The qibla *wall of the Muraykhî mosque (DA 1), Dalmâ.*

in the NE corner. There were three rectangular doorways into the prayer hall from the courtyard, each with a decorative geometric panel above.

The mosque was a very open structure like the other mosques at Dalmâ and mosques in the Gulf area generally, reflecting the need to create ventilation in an extremely hot and humid summer environment in pre-airconditioning days. In the south and the north wall of the prayer hall were four tall, narrow rectangular windows and blind arches above them. In the west (*qibla*) wall, there were six identical windows surmounted by blind arches, three on each side of the *miḥrâb*. In the east wall, there were only two narrow rectangular windows flanking the three entrances.

The centrally situated *miḥrâb* was in the form of a rectangular projection rising nearly the full height of the wall. The *miḥrâb* had rectangular recesses in the upper part of the south, the west and the north walls. These mark the positions of three *bâd gîrr*, mid-wall wind-catchers that served to ventilate the *miḥrâb* interior. The upper part of the *miḥrâb* was roofed by a barrel vault. On the exterior, on the westernmost end of the barrel vault, was a small column, about 1 m. high and 25 cms in diameter with a conical capping.

DA 2

Date: 9.4.92 **Figs:** 25. **Type:** House **Period:** Late Islamic

The house of Muḥammad Jâsim al-Muraykhî was in the centre of a roundabout to the west of the al-Murâykhî Mosque, built by the same Muḥammad Jâsim (DA 1). The house was in two storeys with an arched entrance and fine Gulf-style doors on the ground floor; the post and panel construction was typical of the architecture of the Gulf as a whole, as were the ornamental blind arches. There were two enclosed storage rooms on the ground floor and on the upper floor was an elegant, extremely open room with terraces on each side. Mid-wall wind-catchers and the numerous windows ensured that the building was well ventilated.

Plate 21. The west side of the Muraykhî house (DA 2), Dalmâ.

Plate 22. The interior of the Muraykhî house (DA 2), Dalmâ.

DA 3 **Date:** 1.4.92 **Figs:** 25. **Type:** Mosque **Period:** 1349/1930

Plate 23. Saʿîd Jumʿa al-Qubaysî mosque (DA 3), Dalmâ.

This mosque was situated *ca* 30 m. south of the National Bank of Abu Dhabi in Dalmâ town. The mosque was named after Saʿîd b. Jumʿa al-Qubaysî[14]. The mosque was built of beach stone and coated internally and externally in white plaster. It measured overall 11.6 m. x 10.9 m. It consisted of an open courtyard with a low wall around it, which was bordered on the west (*qibla*) side by the roofed prayer hall. Preceding the prayer hall was a portico, 4 m. deep. An inscription on the *miḥrâb* frame dated it to 1349/1930. At the south-east corner, built against the exterior was an ablution facility.

DA 4 **Date:** 2.4.92 **Figs:** 25. **Type:** Mosque **Period:** Late Islamic

The Saʿîd ʿAlî al-Qubaysî Mosque[15] was situated *ca* 50 m. north of the Dalmâ Co-operative Society, near the al-Muraykhî Pearl House roundabout in Dalmâ. The mosque was constructed of beach rock and covered

Plate 24. Saʿîd ʿAlî Al Qubaysî mosque (DA 4), Dalmâ.

with gypsum plaster: it was whitewashed inside and out. It measured 20.45 m. x 17.5 m. There was an open courtyard on the east side and a flat roofed prayer hall on the west (*qibla*) side. It had a *ḥammâm* at the south-east corner of the courtyard.

Inside the prayer hall there were four central columns supporting the roof, and running parallel to the west wall. The most interesting feature of the mosque was the *miḥrâb,* a recess with a fixed *minbar* built in its north side. There were also blocked mid-wall wind-catchers in the *miḥrâb.*

A striking feature of the mosque is the presence of two fragile pictures of boats incised in plaster on the north side of the portico. These are comparable to boat carvings known from Sirâf and more recently noted in Qaṭar[16].

Date: 1.4.92 **Figs:** 25. **Type:** Burial (?) **Period:** Islamic (?) **DA 5**

This was a rectangular area of disturbed ground south-west of the Muraykhî Pearl House roundabout. The site was 4.5 m. from the road. It was tentatively identified as an Islamic period grave, since it was oriented to 242°, approximately *qibla*. This was very close to the old shore line: all the land to the west of this point has been reclaimed since 1992.

Date: 1.4.92 **Figs:** 25. **Type:** Village settlement **Period:** Late Islamic **DA 6**

Site 6 was in the enclosed area immediately north and NE of the al-Muraykhî Mosque (Site DA 1). This area was pointed out to us as the old centre of Dalmâ town where there had been a large number of houses until about 25 years ago. Now there are gardens and areas of old ground surface showing signs of relatively recent occupation although the original shoreline in this area could be identified. This old occupation area was related both to the al-Muraykhî Pearl House to the south and the cemetery area (Site DA 7) to the north of Site DA 6.

DA 7

UTM 632050°E, 2708160°N.

This important site lay in a fenced area north of Site DA 6, and NE of the Delma Motel roundabout. Access was through Mr Ghassan al-Ghossain's farm on the west side of the enclosure. The site consisted of the old shore-line to the south, rising to higher ground with some bulldozed clearance to the north. The area was especially important as it is undisturbed by building, being an Islamic graveyard of long-standing, whereas the old town areas all around have been either rebuilt or transformed into gardens in recent years.

Plate 25. Settlement area and graveyard (DA 7), Dalmâ.

Fig. 26. Dalmâ: Site DA 7.

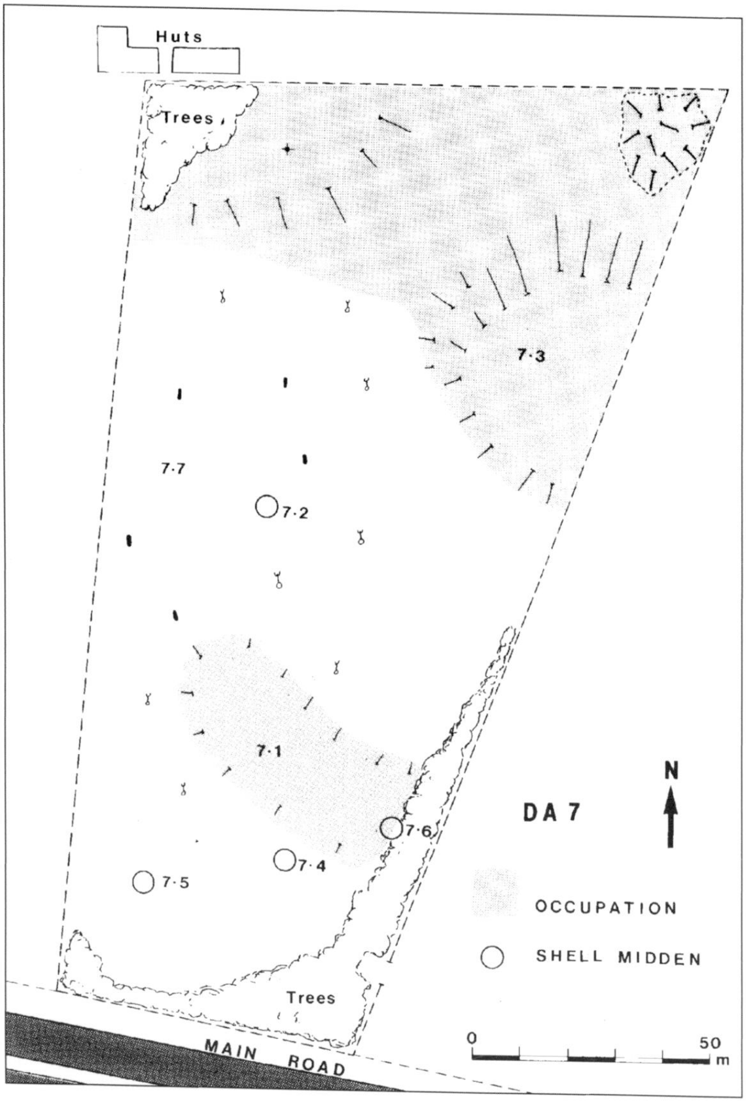

DA 7.1

Date: 1.4.92 **Figs:** 25, 26. **Type:** Occupation mound **Period:** *ca* 6th-7th C. AD-Late Islamic

Site DA 7.1 was the main occupation mound lying NW/SE, measuring approximately 70 m. x 25 m. and about 1 m. high. It stood on a grey sand spit to the south of the higher main shore area of DA 7.3. At some point in the past, lagoon water lay on the land between DA 7.1 and DA 7.3. No pottery or other artefacts were found in these areas.

DA 7.2

Date: 1.4.92 **Figs:** 25, 26. **Type:** Shell midden **Period:** Late Islamic

This shell midden lay between DA 7.1 and DA 7.3, and was approximately 6 m. in diameter and 0.5 m. high. It was disturbed and graves were cut into it.

Date: 1.4.92 **Figs:** 25, 26. **Type:** Shell midden **Period:** *ca* 6th-7th C. AD-Mid. Islamic

DA 7.3

Site DA 7.3 was on the higher ground at the north end of the graveyard. The surface had been bulldozed, especially to the NE. It contained many graves, some of which were recent. Pottery of *ca* 6th C. AD-Early Islamic and mid-Islamic date was scattered over the whole area.

Date: 1.4.92 **Figs:** 25, 26. **Type:** Shell midden **Period:** Islamic (?)

DA 7.4

Site DA 7.4 was a deflated shell midden to the SE of the enclosure, next to the south side of DA 7.1. The midden measured 12 m. x 16 m. and 40 cms height: it was 70% pearl shell and 20% coral.

Date: 1.4.92 **Figs:** 25, 26. **Type:** Shell midden **Period:** Islamic (?)

DA 7.5

Site DA 7.5 was a shell midden in the southern part of the graveyard, 4 m. in diameter and 0.3 m. in height, badly damaged and cut by graves. It consisted of pearl shell and some coral.

Date: 1.4.92 **Figs:** 25, 26. **Type:** Shell midden **Period:** Islamic (?)

DA 7.6

Site DA 7.6 was a low, flattened shell midden at the east end of the graveyard. It was 10 m. in diameter and 0.2 m. high, and it was mostly pearl shell. It had been badly disturbed by gardens encroaching from the east.

Date: 1.4.92 **Figs:** 25, 26. **Type:** Grave **Period:** Late Islamic

DA 7.7

This was a larger Islamic grave. It lay NW of DA 7.2, and between DA 7.1 and DA 7.3. It was oriented to *qibla* at 259°. It had distinctively large head and foot stones. On the NW face of the head stone was inscribed: "al-Shaykh b. Baṭin, 1329" (=1911).

Date: 5.4.92 **Figs:** 25. **Type:** Cemetery **Period:** Islamic

DA 8

UTM 632500° E, 2707715°N.

An elongated walled enclosure surrounded Islamic graves in the centre of Dalmâ, to the east of the old *ṣûq*, and behind the main street and a row of shops. The graves to the west were barely visible, and may have been older than those to the east. There were about 40 rows with 7-14 graves in each. The older group were oriented towards 275-280° while the more recent group were at 262°. We were told that there was formerly a graveyard on the roundabout to the south.

DA 9

Date: 5.4.92 **Figs:** 25. **Type:** Cemetery/occup. area **Period:** Mid-Islamic; Late Islamic

UTM 632775°E, 2707460°N.

Site DA 9 was a rectangular walled graveyard lying between old Dalmâ town and the south island (now joined to the mainland by landfill). It was to the north of the modern *jâmiᶜ*. An area of the old foreshore that preceded modern landfilling was identified here. The foreshore was a continuation of the old shoreline associated with Sites DA 6 and DA 12. The graves at DA 9 were on a higher ridge to the east of the shore and were barely visible as the area was disturbed. The main ceramic concentration was on the ridge to the east. Sherds included mediaeval Islamic and Late Islamic. There were no structural remains.

Plate 26. Occupation area and Islamic graveyard (DA 9), Dalmâ.

DA 10

Date: 5.4.92 **Figs:** 25. **Type:** Islamic cemetery **Period:** Late Islamic

UTM 633065°E, 2706910°N.

Site DA 10 was situated inside the *Jamaᶜiya nahda li-imra'at al-Ẓubyanîya* enclosure against the west wall and at the SE end of Site DA 11. It covered an area measuring 25 m. x 27 m. and it had about 12 graves: only four were clearly visible. Their orientation varied between 250° and 270°. Modern pottery was found.

Date: 5.4.92, 7.4.92 **Figs:** 25, 27. **Type:** Occupation **Period:** ᶜUbaid-related

DA 11

UTM 633010°E, 2707080°N.

Site DA 11 lay in the town of Dalmâ inside the enclosure of the *Jamaᶜiya nahda li-imra'at al-Ẓubyanîya* (The Abu Dhabi Women's Federation). It was situated in the north and west parts of the *Jamaᶜîya* enclosure and appeared to constitute an L-shape, measuring 140 m. x 147 m. and it encompassed both DA 11 and DA 12.1, cumulatively giving a visible area of archaeological deposit of at least 210 m. x 130 m. It lies on old foreshore, preserved by the good fortune of being enclosed within the *Jamaᶜîya* walls.

No structures were noted on the site but this may be because they were of light materials which left no surface indications. There were scatters of flint, many primary flakes, and debitage concentrations and a certain amount of painted ᶜUbaid pottery which supports the apparent date of the flints and beads from the site.

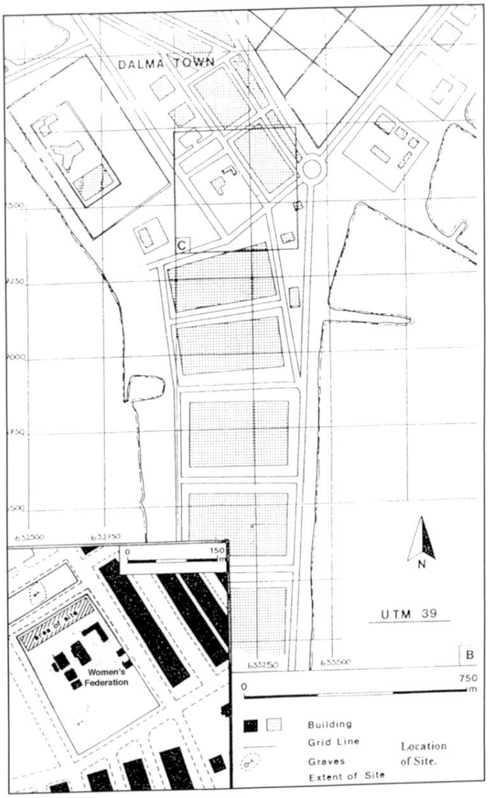

Fig. 27. Dalmâ: Location of site DA 11.

Plate 27. ᶜUbaid-related site in the Jamaᶜîya nahda li-imra'at al-Ẓubyânîya *compound (DA 11), Dalmâ.*

DA 12.1

Date: 5.4.92 **Figs:** 25. **Type:** Occupation **Period:** ʿUbaid-relatiod; Late Islamic

UTM 6329980°E, 2707125°N.

This site was a part of DA 11. It was also on old shoreline with occupation debris immediately south of the rectangular enclosure of the *Jamaʿiya nahda li-imra'at al-Ẓubyanîya* compound. The occupation area measured overall 120 m. x 47 m. on a traffic island between the twin asphalted lanes of a dual carriageway. The centre of the site had an elevation of about 40 cms, suggesting that there may be some stratigraphy to the site, even though it has been very disturbed by Late Islamic graves and modern road building. Areas of flint knapping were noted throughout the area. Like the related site DA 11, DA 12.1 was associated with an ʿUbaid-related settlement.

DA 12.2

Date: 5.4.92 **Figs:** 25. **Type:** Cemetery **Period:** Late Islamic

UTM 6329980°E, 2707125°N.

Site DA 12.1 was to the north of DA 12.2. It was a raised area measuring 40 m. x 30 m. with groups of irregularly oriented graves which appeared to be Islamic. They had small head and foot stones and had been disturbed by trees.

DA 13

Date: 7.4.92 **Figs:** 25. **Type:** Village occupation **Period:** Late Islamic

UTM 631705°E, 2708320°N.

Site DA 13 was an elongated area situated on the old shoreline NW of the Delma Motel roundabout between the twin tarmac roads that lead to President Zayed's palace. It was a continuation of the foreshore noted

Plate 28. Islamic occupation area at Abû'l-ʿUmâma (DA 13), Dalmâ.

at Site DA 7, with a lagoon area lying between. It was the site of a former village lying SE of the rocky outcrop known as Abû'l-ᶜUmâma because it looks like a turban *(ᶜumâma)*. The maximum area was *ca* 250 m. x 50 m. The least disturbed area was to the south and SE of the Abû'l-ᶜUmâma outcrop. There were scatters of Late Islamic pottery from the Julfâr horizon but no architectural remains were visible on the surface. This was said to have been the site of one of two villages that once stood in this area, the second being al-Biyâḍa (Site DA 16) on the SW side of the island.

To the NW of Abû'l-ᶜUmâma there were once two cemeteries, one of which is said to have been for children. Our local informants recalled that a very large ceramic vessel, in excess of 1 m. high, was found near these cemetery areas.

Date: 7.4.92, 7.4.92 **Figs:** 25, 28. **Type:** Cistern & enclosure **Period:** Islamic

DA 14

Plate 29. Cistern and palm tree stand (DA 14), Dalmâ.

Fig. 28. Dalmâ: Site DA 14.

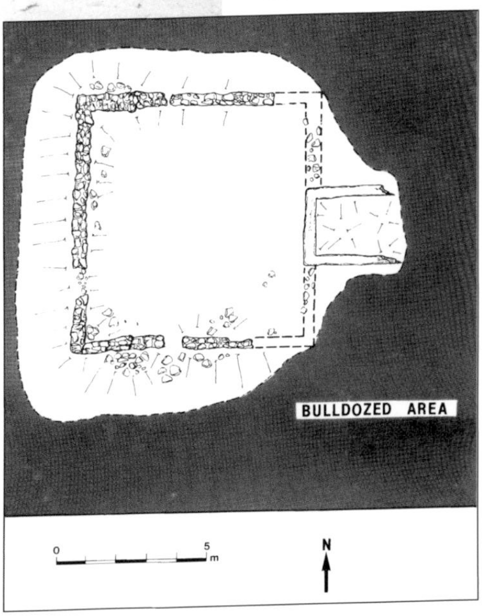

UTM 632450°E, 2708180°N.

The site was to the east of the outskirts of Dalmâ, beyond a football pitch and gardens in this area, and south of a group of gas tanks. There was a great deal of bulldozed material in the area. It had probably been an enclosed palm-grove, for there were the remains of a rough beach-rock enclosure wall measuring 8.5 m. N/S and 8.1 m. E/W, surviving on the north, west and south sides; the west side alone was intact, standing to a height of 70 cms. The cistern measured 2.5 m. N/S x 3 m. E/W, with enclosing walls 25 cms wide. It was filled with rubble and the depth of the tank could not be estimated.

DA 15 **Date:** 6.4.92 **Figs:** 25. **Type:** Well **Period:** Islamic (?)

UTM 630230°E, 2709185°N.

This was a large well, whose name was given to us as al-Falaj, situated 2.1 km north of the Delma Motel on the west side of the island: it lay 5 m. east of the coastal road. It was overgrown by trees and was once used by passing boats for water. Local people said that water ran into it from a "cave" on one side.

DA 16 **Date:** 6.4.92 **Figs:** 25. **Type:** Village **Period:** Late Islamic

UTM 630025°E, 2710185°N.

This was the site of a late Islamic village known as al-Biyâḍa, situated on the west side of Dalmâ, 0.7 km from the Delma Motel roundabout. The site had been bulldozed and no remains survived except beachrock, broken shells and flint nodules spread over an area *ca* 200 m. x 100 m. When a smallpox outbreak struck three generations ago, the survivors from al-Biyâḍa moved to the village at site DA 13 beside Abû'l-ᶜUmâma and the old town centre of Dalmâ (Site DA 6).

DA 17.1 **Date:** 11.4.92 **Figs:** 25, 29. **Type:** Graves **Period:** Islamic (?)

UTM 630420°E, 2710430°N.

This was a burial site situated *ca* 2 kms inland from a red buoy floating off the western shore of the island: the burials were located on the flood plain of a wadi in an area of volcanic outcrops. There were three graves grouped together, and there was a fourth possible grave. The graves were hard to recognise because there were so many low volcanic mounds in this area.

Grave 1 was on a circular sandy mound 4 m. x 4 m., with a central rectangular burial rising to about 70 cms; it lay N/S to *qibla* at 278°. There seemed to be a stone kerb and foot- and head-stones at each end, about 45 cms high.

Grave 2 was a low sub-rectangular mound, 4 m. x 1.50 m. and 50 cms high, lying N/S on a *qibla* orientation of 270°. Some of the stones may have been natural volcanic outcroppings.

Grave 3 was again sub-rectangular, measuring 3.50 m. x 1 m., standing to about *ca* 15 cms; the headstones and footstones stood to *ca* 50 cms. The orientation was to NW/SE, to *qibla* at 220°.

Grave 4 was far more uncertain and may have been natural. It lay some distance SE of the large graves 1-3, on the north side of a track. It was rectangular, measuring 1 m. x 1.5 m., on an E/W orientation, towards

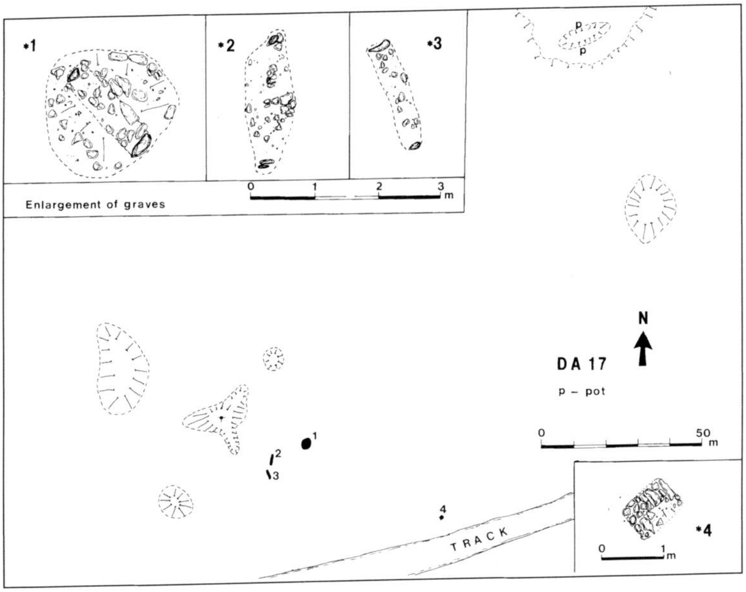

Fig. 29. Dalmâ: Site DA 17.

230° and rising to *ca* 20 cms. It did not seem to be Islamic, if indeed it was a grave at all.

The rectangular form and orientations of Graves 1-3 suggests that they are all Islamic, but they were unusually large. We were shown this site by Mr Saᶜîd al-Muraykhî. Mr Eid al-Mazrûᶜî's father had visited the site about 1972 with foreigners from al-ᶜAyn, whom, he said, had collected pottery from the site. We found no pottery at the graves.

Date: 11.4.92, 7.4.92 **Figs:** 25, 29. **Type:** Sherd scatter **Period:** Mid-Islamic **DA 17.2**

UTM 630420°E, 2710430°N.

Site DA 17.2 lay NE of DA 17.1 at a distance of about 160 m. It consisted of two separate sherd scatters on the north side of the wadi flood plain, 5 m. apart. The smaller group covered only 60 cms. x 40 cms; the larger group covered 1.5 m. x 2 m. and included a whole but broken vessel.

Date: 6.4.92, 7.4.92 **Figs:** 25. **Type:** Excavation site **Period:** *ca* 5th-8th C.? **DA 18**

UTM 632455°E, 2709000°N.

Site DA 18 was on the south side of the island in the low hills immediately north of Dalmâ town. It was approached by the graded road running north beside the Shaᶜba Ḥazîm *falaj* tanks (Site DA 22). The site was situated on a rocky slope of volcanic lava on the east bank of a wadi running from the north, and about 200 m. from the southern mouth of the wadi. We were told that this was where excavations by an Iraqi team had taken place in 1973. This site was noted by Cleuziou and described as Sassanian-early Islamic. There is now no trace of the excavated area which has been obliterated by bulldozing. We were told that it was once the site of stone buildings. We have been unable to locate any report from the Iraqi excavation.

DA 19 **Date:** 6.4.92 **Figs:** 25. **Type:** Well **Period:** Islamic (?)

UTM 630790°E, 2712685°N.

Site DA 19 was a large spring or well known as al-Faḥaḥil, 5.85 kms north of the Delma Motel roundabout on the west side of the island. It lay 100 m. west of the coast road, and it was not far from the base of a cliff to the east. It was said to have been used by boats as a watering place. When we saw it, the well was only a muddy area about 5 m. in diameter. Site DA 19.2 lay to the SW.

DA 19.2 **Date:** 6.4.92 **Figs:** 25. **Type:** Graves **Period:** Islamic

UTM 630790°E, 2712685°N.

This site was a group of three to four Islamic graves to the SW of the well, site DA 19.1. The area had been partly bulldozed.

DA 20 **Date:** 7.4.92 **Figs:** 25. **Type:** Stone scatter **Period:** Islamic

UTM 632090°E, 2708640°N.

Site DA 20 lay on the south side of the island, just north of Dalmâ town. It was west of site DA 18 and west of two large silver tanks. The tanks and site DA 20 were once on the same hill, but bulldozing has separated them. Residents of Dalmâ showed us the site and recalled that there was a simple mosque here until about 1987, outlined by stones about 30 m. long and standing 50 cms high. There had been a *miḥrâb* recess in the centre. This mosque had vanished, although we found a disturbed line of stones where it had been. To the east were scatters of pottery and pearl oyster shell and to the SW were further scatters of pottery.

DA 21 **Date:** 6.4.92 **Figs:** 25. **Type:** Industrial site **Period:** Islamic (?)

UTM 633370°E, 2709075°N.

This site was on the south side of the island on the SE edge of the foothills north of the town of Dalmâ. The site was east of Shaʿba Ḥazîm, and immediately below a conical hill called Jarn al-Safâfîr: there was a steel mast to the east.

Plate 30. Iron smelting site (DA 21), Dalmâ.

The site was situated on an irregular platform of purple rock, roughly 50 m. x 40 m. standing 1.5 m. above a wadi bed. Into this platform, three to five sub-oval holes had been bored and back-filled. One of these to the NE was 3 m. deep and about 3 m. x 2 m. wide at the mouth: another was 1 m. x 1 m. There were also five spoil heaps. On the platform were scattered, small iron nodules. According to local informants, iron smithing had taken place at the site, using iron from Dalmâ, although the iron did not necessarily originate at this spot. The smelting took place at this area because it was away from the settlements around Dalmâ and the ground was level. We were told that there used to be iron rings for tethering horses set into the rocks, but none of these remained. There were no finds apart from iron nodules.

We were told by Mûsâ b. Râshid that Labatt Co.(?) mined iron ore in 1951 for a period of five to six months and that the ore was carried by a light railway track down to the port for shipping. There is no trace of this track now.

Date: 11.4.92, 7.4.92 **Figs:** 25. **Type:** Wells **Period:** Islamic (?)

DA 22

This site lay on the south side of the island, beyond the northern outskirts of Dalmâ town, to the east of site DA 7 and SE of site DA 20. It consisted of four wells, three of which were surrounded by round concrete structures, and the fourth was surrounded by a square structure, all added in the modern period. They were termed *falaj* Ḥazîm: they took this name from the wadi called Shaʿba Ḥazîm to the north. However, the

Plate 31. Falaj *tanks at Wâdî Ḥazîm (DA 22), Dalmâ.*

term falaj seems to be incorrect and to the best of our estimate, all were wells. There were no old structures on the surface nor were there any finds. Water was at 2.50 m. depth from the surface before rain, but it rose after rainfall to only 1.8 m. below the surface.

Notes

1 Freya Stark (*The Coast of Incense. Autobiography, 1933-1939*, London (1953), p. 134) confirms this trade in water, referring to an unfinished *sambûq* that she visited in Kuwait which was being built specifically to carry water between al-Baṣra and Kuwait. Ms S. al-Mutawa has informed me that her grandmother in Kuwait preferred water imported from al-Baṣra even after Kuwait had introduced piped local water. Captain Maarten Verhage who knows the waters off the UAE coast told me in March, 1995 that water for Abu Dhabi and elsewhere used to be towed in large wooden containers behind boats. This evidence of a local water trade corresponds to the situation at the island of New Hurmûz, where sweet water was imported. Of lesser significance is the fact that the British forces campaigning against the Âl Qâsimî brought water from India, but this was dictated by military need.

2 Slot, *op. cit.*, p. 38.

3 Buckingham, *op. cit.*, p. 450.

4 Brucks, *op. cit.*, section III, p. 554.

5 J. Harsburgh, op *op. cit.*, Section III, p. 248.

6 Lorimer, *op. cit.*,IIA, p. 409.

7 Lorimer, *op. cit.*,IIA, p. 363.

8 According to Peter Hellyer, this trade continued until shortly after World War II.

9 *op. cit.*, pp. 188-9.

10 B. Vogt, W. Gockel, H. Hofbauer and A.A. al-Haj, *op. cit.*, p. 50.

11 S. Cleuziou in G. Harter *et al.*, pp. 10-12. I am indebted to Dr C. Hardy-Guilbert for sending a copy of Cleuziou's paper.

12 I take it that this is the site excavated by the Iraqis.

13 J. Beaucamp and C. Robin, "L'évêche nestorien de Mâsmâhig dans l'archipel d'al-Bahrayn (Ve-IXe siècle)", *Dilmun. New Studies in the Archaeology and Early History of Bahrain* , ed. D.T. Potts, Berlin (1983), *Band* 2, pp. 171-196.

14 By 1995, after restoration, a name plaque gave the name of the mosque as *masjid al-Qubaysât*.

15 After restorations in 1994, a plaque now names the mosque after Saᶜîd ᶜAlî al-Muhannadî.

16 D. Whitehouse, "Excavations at Sirâf", *Iran* x (1972), pp. 74-5.
The Qaṭar examples have been discussed most recently by W. Facey, "The Boat Carvings at Jabal Jusasiyya, N.E. Qatar", *Proceedings of the Seminar for Arabian Studies* 17 (1987), pp. 199-222.

MARAWAḤ (MR)

Marawaḥ is at UTM 732500°E/ 2687000°N on the north side of the Khawr al-Bazam. This is a long channel that opens from the west and runs between the mainland and the chain of islands, reefs and shoals to which Marawaḥ belongs. Marawaḥ is very low lying and is about 13 kms from east to west and 5.5 kms from north to south at its widest point. At the western end is the island of Liffiya, separated from Marawaḥ by a narrow channel: at low tide local people report that it is possible to cross between the two islands, even by car.

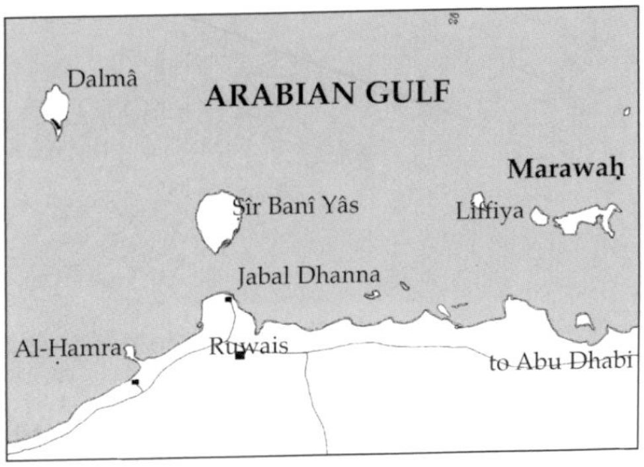

Apart from the recent buildings constructed by HE Shaykh Muḥammad b. Zayed, there are three small former population centres; Liffa in the west, overlooking the island of Liffiya; Ghubba (sometimes recorded as Ghurbah) on the long southern bay of the island; and Marawaḥ at the eastern end of the island.

There is seasonal occupation down to the present day by fishermen at all three settlements. We met a number of people living on Liffiya, although the old villages on Marawaḥ were all deserted at the time of our visit.

The island is mentioned, although not as Marawaḥ, in the British navigational records, based on the East India Company nautical surveys of the early decades of the 19th century. Probably because of the difficulty of approaching Marawaḥ, the British accounts say very little of it, and subsume it into their general reports on the reefs and islands that run

Plate 32. Western Marawaḥ (left) with the settlement of Liffa and the island of Liffiya (right). Site MR 1 is on the coast at centre picture.

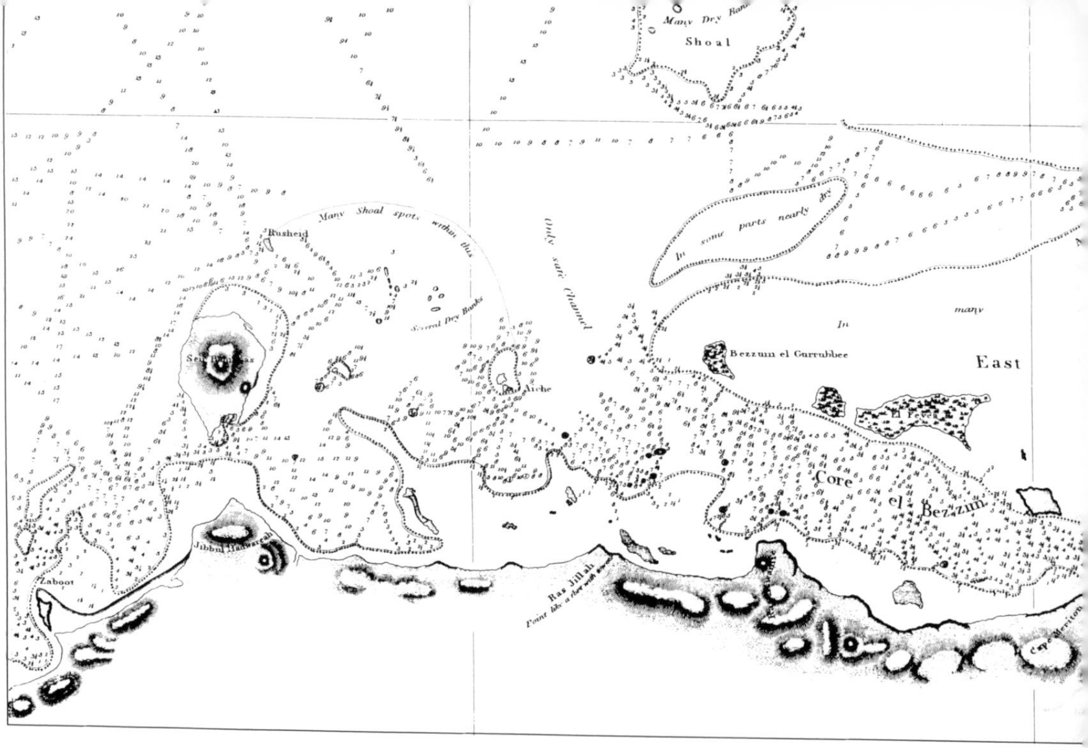

Fig. 30. *Khawr al-Bazm and "El Feyea". (India Office Library and Records, ORW 1990a 1379, Chart 8).*

along the northern side of the Khawr al-Bazam. However, they all speak of the dangers of navigation in this area. The islands on the north side of the Khawr, including Marawaḥ, were known to early British navigators as the "East India Company's Islands"[1].

Captain George Brucks, writing in 1829 in the earliest reference to the islands, says the following:

> *EAST INDIA COMPANY'S ISLAND*
>
> *East India Company's Islands from Jazeerat Jehnany* [Junayna, Juneina], *southern point in lat. 24° 10′ 35″ ″ N., long. 53° 38′E. in Bezzim el Gurabee* [Bazam al-Gharbî immediately west of Marawaḥ], *the western in lat. 24° 18′ 40″ N., long 53° 12′ 10″ E., consist of Jehnany, three others without names, and Bezzim el Gurabee. These, with Jazeerat Billyaird* [Abû'l-Abyad] *and the reefs, which connect the whole with each other from the northern side of Khore el Bezzim, and on the outside from the inshore channel, are low, in some parts rocky, and most of them covered with wood, but none of them contain any water.*
>
> *KHORE EL BEZZIM*
>
> *Khore el Bezzim is formed on the northern side by East India Company's Islands, and on the south by the mainland of Arabia, and is forty miles deep from its entrance at Bezzim el Gurabee, and from five miles at the entrance to one at the upper part wide, having soundings from nine to two fathoms at the upper part. The deepest water and best channel is about one-third over from the islands, near the main. Several small patches, with one and a half and two fathoms, lay scattered about. This place is said to have been one of*

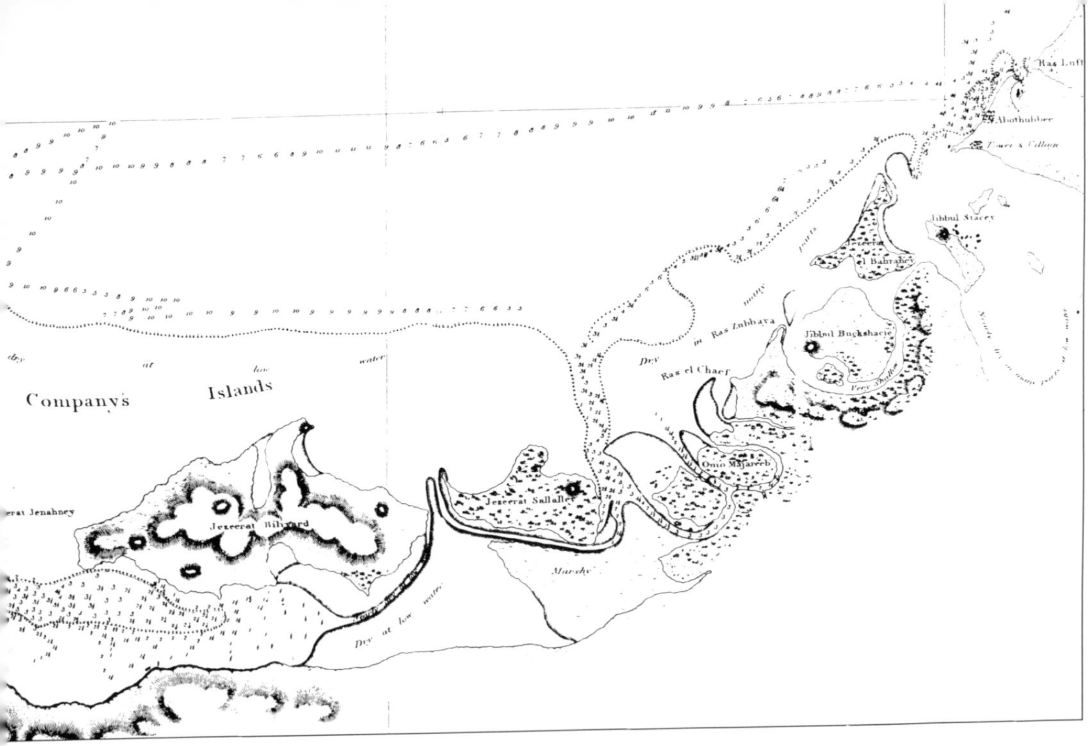

the resorts of the pirates, and many of their boats were said to have been here at the time of the expedition [i.e., the British expedition against the Âl Qâsimî in 1819]."

Further on, the following comments are added on navigating the Khawr al-Bazam:

Unless in case of necessity, or being in chase, no vessel should come in here, in which case I can only recommend great attention to the lead and look-out, as the only guides they can have. After passing the sandy island of Aiche [ᶜIsh] *in lat. 24° 17′ 30″ N., long. 53° 1′ 35″ E., when, if running for Khore el Bezzim, run in as near mid-channel, between the island of Bezzim el Gurabee and the main, as possible, keeping a sharp look-out for a small shoal patch bearing run W. five and a half miles from the body of the island. After passing, steer boldly up the Khore, keeping near mid-channel until you near the fourth island, when haul for it, and keep about one-fifth over from it towards the main to clear a shoal patch on that side.*

Brucks's account requires some clarification[2]. The westernmost island on the north side of the Khawr al-Bazam channel is Bazam al-Gharbî, followed by Marawaḥ, and then al-Junayna. Brucks records three islands between Bazam al-Gharbî and al-Junayna, whereas there are only two, Liffiya and Marawaḥ. It is likely that, because of the shallows off Marawaḥ, British boats never approached close enough to perceive that it is one island rather than two: furthermore, as we have seen, at low tide it is possible to drive across to Liffiya from Marawaḥ, reinforcing the impression of a single island. The fourth island to which Brucks recommended navigators to haul as they pressed up the Khawr al-Bazam was probably Marawaḥ.

The same waters were described in *The India Directory* of 1891[3]:

> *THE COAST, to the S. and W. of Abu Zhabi, changes to a W. direction, and is fronted by a chain of islands, formerly called East India Company's Islands, but each of them has a native name. The chain extends parallel with the coast in an E. and W. direction, from the meridian of Abu Zhabi to Khor-el-Besm, and is surrounded by an unbroken line of coral reefs, and shoal water extends many miles off them.*

As late as 1938, *The Persian Gulf Pilot* was still unaware of the name Marawaḥ and effectively repeated the information in the 1891 *India Directory*[4]. Speaking of the Bazam reef on the north side of the Khawr al-Bazm, the following is recorded:

> *A chain of islands, usually called collectively Bazam, though each island has its own proper name, extends along the southern edge of the reef. All the islands are waterless.*

The easternmost islands are recorded as Jazîrat Salâlî, followed by Abû'l-Abyaḍ and al-Junayna. Beyond a rocky islet, near al-Junayna, was "Al Fiha".

> *Al Fiha (Lat. 24° 17′ N., Long. 53° 16′ E.) is a low island, situated about 9 miles westward of Al Junaina, close westward of which is another; both lie on the southern side of the reef.*

Beyond again was Bazam al-Gharbî, the westernmost of the Bazam reef islands. Marawaḥ lies in the identical position to the *Persian Gulf Pilot*'s "Al Fiha". This name is clearly a corruption of Liffiya, the island at the western tip of Marawaḥ. The *Pilot* recognizes that they were two separate islands, but the name of the small island of Liffiya has been transferred to Marawaḥ as a whole.

In June 1990, a party from the Emirates Natural History Group studied the natural history of Marawaḥ and produced a report for HE Shaykh Muḥammad b. Zayed Al Nahyan. This report included a section on the archaeology of the island[5]. The authors of the report noted remains of huts and shell mounds at both Ghubba and the eastern settlement known as Marawaḥ, with an especially large mound at the latter. Near Liffa at the west end they recorded a building which they took to be a mosque. Until the ADIAS team visited Marawaḥ, this was the limit of archaeological work on the island.

Our own investigations in 1992 showed that Marawaḥ is an island of considerable archaeological interest with a large Late Stone Age lithic site (MR 1) which is a significant addition to the very early archaeological sites known in the United Arab Emirates. It is a site that should be investigated further and protected in the meantime. There are also a number of other sites on the island which may be related to MR 1 and which should also be examined in the future.

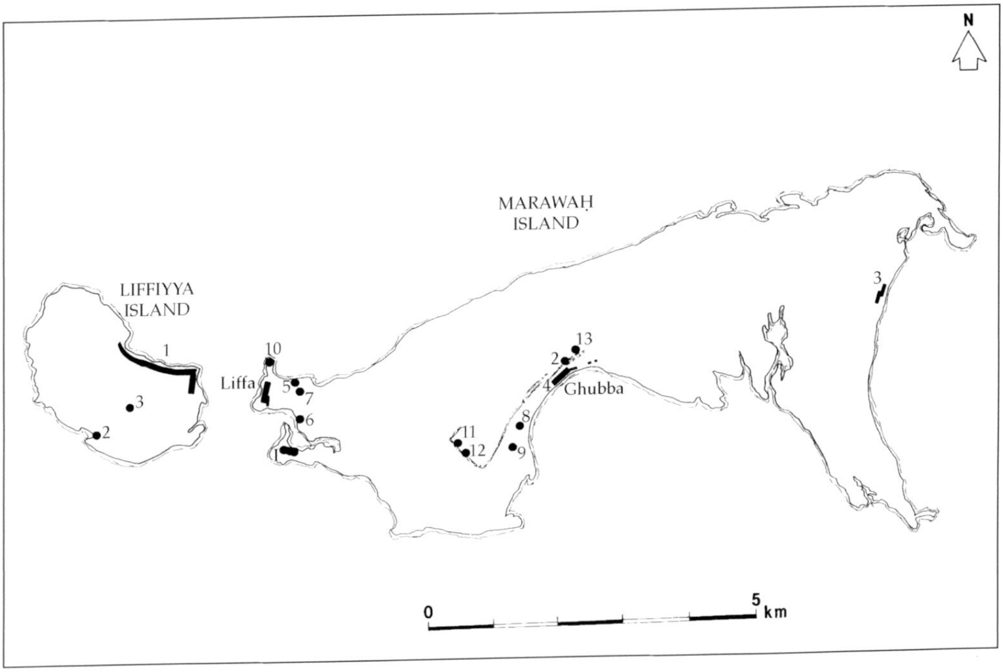

Fig. 31. Marawaḥ: Site location.

THE SITES

Date: 15.4.92 **Figs:** 31. **Type:** Occupation **Period:** Late Stone Age **MR 1.1-1.10**

The site stood on a low, rocky coastal promontory at the SW end of Marawaḥ, about 2 kms to the south of the village of Liffa. The site overlooked a bay and the terrain provided one of the few places on the coast with any elevation. The area as a whole was described to us as Liffa.

Plate 33. General view of Late Stone Age site (MR 1), Marawaḥ, looking WSW.

The site was situated on a limestone plateau *ca* 500 m. x 200 m. It was covered with lithics that reflected Late Stone Age occupation and perhaps later activity. A total of 54 separate elements were identified within the overall site MR 1, consisting of several mounds, wall lines and rectangular structural traces. Cleared spaces suggested campsites, and there were also cairns, oval depressions, stone rings, artefact scatters and debitage. The numerous elements of the site reflected its excellent state of preservation and its lack of disturbance.

The profusion of arrow-heads, knives, scrapers and piercers in the lithic assemblage collected at the site suggested that the plateau was associated with hunting and fishing in the Late Stone Age. The location gave easy access for catching fish, dugong and crustaceans.

MR 2

MR 2 lay to the north and east of the village of Ghubba at a distance of about 0.5 km. It consisted of a series of sites distributed on the east/west limestone ridges: without exception, the sites observed were on top of the ridges which constituted old shorelines and outcrops. No sites or artefacts were found on the sandy depressions which were once coastal plain and old beaches between the ridges. It is possible that the MR 2 sites were unrelated spatially and temporally.

MR 2.1

Date: 15.4.92 **Figs:** 31. **Type:** Cistern **Period:** Islamic (?)

Site MR 2.1 was a cistern measuring *ca* 60 cms x 40 cms and it was about 25 cms deep, but filled with silt. There were at least two cut channels following the slope of the rock outcrop, draining rainwater run-off into the cistern.

MR 2.2

Date: 15.4.92 **Figs:** 31. **Type:** Water Jar **Period:** Late Islamic

This site was marked by a large, buff-coloured, coarse gritted water jar, *ca* 80 cms tall, *ca* 50 cms+ in maximum girth, lying on its side in a shallow depression, *ca* 1.5 m. in diameter and *ca* 50 cms deep. Water collects here in wet weather. Late Islamic sherds were collected from the same area.

MR 2.3

Date: 15.4.92 **Figs:** 31. **Type:** Water collection system (?) **Period:** Islamic (?)

The site was on an outcrop north of the main ridge. A small crescent of stones *ca* 1 m. in diameter abutted two natural boulders forming a small enclosure on the plateau on top of the outcrop. It was possibly a water collection system.

MR 2.4

Date: 15.4.92 **Figs:** 31. **Type:** **Period:** ?

The site was a double ring of stones at the eastern end of a shallow depression filled with silty sand. The outer ring was *ca* 2 m. in diameter in the outer ring; the inner ring was *ca* 40 cms in diameter. The function of the double stone ring was unclear.

MR 2.5

Date: 15.4.92 **Figs:** 31. **Type:** **Period:** Pre-Islamic (?)

This site was a collapsed cairn at the west end of a small central ridge, *ca* 4 m. x 3 m. and *ca* 1.5 m. high: it had a possible kerb. It may be related to MR 2.6.

Date: 15.4.92 **Figs:** 31. **Type:** Stone wall **Period:** Late Stone Age (?) **MR 2.6**

At this site there was a single course limestone wall running E.-W. There was a cleared sandy space about 4 m. to the south. Shelter was provided to the east by an outcrop of bedrock. The site was identified as a possible camp site. Finds included a broken tanged arrowhead.

MR 3

The coastal village known as Marawaḥ on the east side of the island was 4.52 kms north of the modern residential complex built by Shaykh Muḥammad. Marawaḥ was deserted at the time of the survey and consisted of wooden shacks on the east side of track. The beach was lined by mangroves along the high water mark. There were also two fish traps on the long tidal beach. A distinctive shack had white water tanks on its roof. There were a number of shell middens and pearl shell scatters in the area north of the village. Some Late Islamic to recent pottery was noted. There were deflated middens further north which could be earlier.

Date: 13.4.92 **Figs:** 31. **Type:** Shell middens **Period:** Late Islamic **MR 3.1**

There were several low shell middens covered in dune sand, near high water mark to the SE of Marawaḥ village.

Date: 13.4.92 **Figs:** 31. **Type:** Shell middens **Period:** Late Islamic **MR 3.2-3.11**

To the north of the village were a series of ten large shell middens and a smaller shell scatter, lying between 10 m.-40 m. from HWM. With the exception of MR 3.7 and 3.11, they all contained 85-95% pearl oyster shell and other debris relating to pearling activities in the Late Islamic to modern period. Several middens also had ash deposits. The more recent middens were the more southerly group, closest to the village. The more deflated and possibly earlier middens were further to the north.

MR 4

Site MR 4 was a large village known as Ghubba on the south side of the island. It ran along the sea front with its shacks and huts dating from at least 50 years ago down to the recent period. There were fourteen shell middens near the shore and an interesting group of traditional buildings including a mosque at the east end of the village (MR 4.8-4.11). There was fish bone and shell but little pottery around the MR 4.8-4.11 group. Inland were several other occupation areas (MR 4.5-4.7), and sites MR 2 and MR 13 lay north and may be associated with Ghubba.

MR 4.1

Date: 14.4.92 **Figs:** 31. **Type:** Midden **Period:** Late Islamic/recent

This was a particularly large midden close to the shore and measuring 26 m. E/W and 21 m. N/S with a covering of *Murex* shells, pottery and other modern material. Between MR 4.1 and the shore was further shell detritus (mainly *Murex* shells and also turtle carapaces) and unevenly spread pottery scatters.

MR 4.2

Date: 14.4.92 **Figs:** 31. **Type:** Midden **Period:** Late Islamic

Site MR 4.2 was another large midden, 20 m. west of MR 4.1, measuring 20 m. E/W and 36 m. N/S with a heavy covering of *Murex* shells on the NE side and dugong bones concentrated in the centre and to the west. There were quantities of red unglazed pottery and incised buff-wares, and some glass.

MR 4.3

Date: 14.4.92 **Figs:** 31. **Type:** Middens **Period:** Late Islamic

Site MR 4.3 was a series of six middens, 120 m. NE of two buildings near MR 4.1, and *ca* 50 m. north of HWM, varying from 3 m. diameter to 15 m. x 8 m. The largest midden was 95% pearl oyster shell and had late 19th century glass. Some of the middens appeared to be older.

MR 4.4

Date: 14.4.92 **Figs:** 31. **Type:** Middens **Period:** Late Islamic/recent

This site consisted of a group of five middens east of MR 4.1 with mixed shells, pottery and some iron fragments. There was also a butchery site with the (recent) skeleton of an adult and a baby dugong to the east.

MR 4.5

Date: 14.4.92 **Figs:** 31. **Type:** Occupation **Period:** Late Islamic/recent

Site MR 4.5 was north of Ghubba on a ridge lying 150 m. NW of MR 4.1 and 4.2. The ridge was one of a series running in a curve, parallel to the shore: beyond to the north were MR 13 and MR 2.

At a point where the ridge was 10 m. across, there was a low wall. There was also a scatter of pottery, glass, deteriorated iron and bone, with more modern material nearer Ghubba. Just before the track traversed MR 4.5, there was an outline structure similar to MR 4.6.

MR 4.6

Date: 14.4.92 **Figs:** 31. **Type:** Occupation **Period:** Late Islamic (?)

MR 4.6 was west of MR 4.5. There were a series of "wall lines" marked out by single stones laid to define small rectangular "rooms", sometimes with openings indicated.

Date: 14.4.92 **Figs:** 31. **Type:** Occupation **Period:** Islamic (?) **MR 4.7**

2 m. SW of the track was a mound measuring 14 m. N/S and 5 m. E/W with wall traces similar to those at MR 4.6. There was no pottery.

Date: 14.4.92 **Figs:** 31. **Type:** House **Period:** Late Islamic **MR 4.8**

This was a courtyard house in the eastern part of Ghubba and one of several buildings of some interest in terms of the indigenous later Islamic building tradition. It was built of re-used wood from a diversity of sources and it measured 18 m. x 15 m. It had a single entrance on the SW side towards the sea which gave on to an open courtyard. Wooden rooms ran around three sides (SW, NW, and NE). The roofing of the rooms was pitched. At the NW corner was a room whose walls were formed by an open lattice, which was taken to be summer sleeping quarters. A room on the NE side of the courtyard with embroidered pillows around the wall was taken to have been the men's *majlis*. A kitchen stood in the north corner of the enclosure and a further (women's?) *majlis* was on NW side.

Date: 14.4.92 **Figs:** 31. **Type:** Mosque **Period:** Late Islamic **MR 4.9**

Immediately SW of house MR 4.8 was a mosque built in an identical manner with re-used wood. The mosque was oriented to *qibla* at 260° and it measured 8 m. x 9 m. overall. It had a chamber on the NE side measuring 9 m. x 2.5 m. which had open wooden lattice walls to create as cool an environment as possible in the heat of the region. A closed prayer hall lay behind it to the SE, measuring 5.5 m. x 9 m. with a rectangular *miḥrâb* in the centre of the *qibla* wall.

Plate 34. Wooden mosque (MR 4.9) at Ghubba, Marawaḥ.

Plate 35. Miḥrâb *of the wooden mosque (MR 4.9) at Ghubba, Marawaḥ.*

MR 4.10 **Date:** 14.4.92 **Figs:** 31. **Type:** Boat house **Period:** Late Islamic

Immediately south of the mosque was a wooden boat-house measuring 8 m. x 3 m.

MR 4.11 **Date:** 14.4.92 **Figs:** 31. **Type:** Building **Period:** Late Islamic

To the south of the mosque, beside the boat-house was a building used as a store for fishing nets.

Date: 14.4.92 **Figs:** 31, 32. **Type:** Mosque **Period:** Late Islamic **MR 5**

There was a late mosque less than 1 km east of the village of Liffa, immediately north of the track that ran from the village along the north side of the island. It measured 11 m. x 4.8 m. and it was built of beach-rock with the lower 80 cms of cut masonry and the upper part of rougher stone: there was no mortar. Like mosques of similar character elsewhere in the region (*e.g.* the mosque on Ṣîr Banî Yâs, Site SBY 10), it has no superstructure and it was designed as such, with its walls standing only to 1.5 m. There are 50 cm square recesses set in the walls at about 85 cms above ground level. These were for *Qur'âns*, one of which was still *in situ*. The *miḥrâb* formed a rectangular projection in the centre of the western (*qibla*) wall, which was oriented to 276°: it was built of very large panels of beach-rock. The mosque was probably related to the cemetery (MR 7) to the SE.

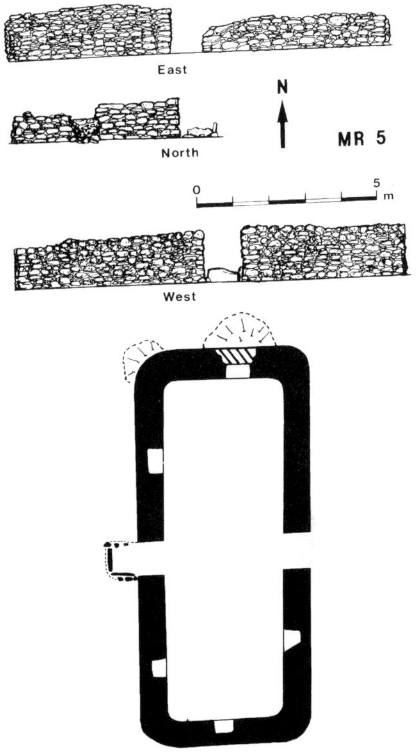

Fig. 32. Marawaḥ: Mosque: Site MR 5.

Plate 36. Open mosque (MR 5) east of Liffa, Marawaḥ.

MR 6 **Date:** 15.4.92 **Figs:** 31. **Type:** Cairns **Period:** ?

There was a group of four cairns on the west coast of Marawaḥ, *ca* 1 km south of Liffa village, on the old coast line above the *sabkha* (salt flats). These cairns lay east of MR 1. There was considerable doubt about these cairns which were probably partly modern; no finds were located and there were modern falcon perches on top of two of them (MR 6.1 and 6.4). However, there may be ancient cairns beneath and they should be re-examined.

MR 7

This cemetery area lay *ca* 200 m. SE of the mosque (MR 5) outside Liffa.

MR 7.1 **Date:** 15.4.92 **Figs:** 31. **Type:** Cemetery **Period:** Islamic

This was a recent Islamic grave site with *ca* 40 burials, with rectangular stone outlines, headstones and footstones. The kerbs had been robbed out.

MR 7.2 **Date:** 15.4.92 **Figs:** 31. **Type:** Burial **Period:** Pre-Islamic

This site was a collapsed cairn 24 m. north of the Islamic graves, measuring 3.95 m. in diameter.

MR 7.3 **Date:** 15.4.92 **Figs:** 31. **Type:** Burial **Period:** Pre-Islamic

A collapsed stone circle lying 49 m. north of MR 7.2, 3.90 m. in diameter.

MR 8 **Date:** 16.4.92 **Figs:** 31. **Type:** Wells **Period:** Late Islamic (?)

The site was about 1 km west of Ghubba and *ca* 1 km inland from a mangrove stand, south of a sandy ridge. There were about six wells each about 60 cms in diameter, in an area about 30 m. E/W and 40 m. N/S. Water was found in three of the wells at *ca* 1.5 m. depth below the ground surface. There was a single palm tree.

MR 9 **Date:** 16.4.92 **Figs:** 31. **Type:** Hearths (?) **Period:** Islamic (?)

This site was to the SW of Ghubba and *ca* 0.3 km west of site MR 8. There were six stone features, and possibly eight altogether in an area measuring 47 m. E/W and 17 m. N/S. They were tentatively identified as hearths. Two of them had oblong kerbs, and they lay on a N/S orientation, measuring 1.5 m. x 70 cms. Four were circular and oval, with varying diameters of 1 m., 1.3 m., 1.5 m., and 2 m. Their maximum height was 40 cms.

Date: 15.4.92 **Figs:** 31. **Type:** Midden **Period:** Late Islamic **MR 10**

At the far NW point of the island on a promontory towards Liffiya, there was a small midden, measuring *ca* 1 m. in diameter which was collapsing down a small cliff on the north side. There were crab and turtle shells and dugong bones scattered on the surface. This promontory appears to have been used as a landing place for fishing boats.

Date: 16.4.92 **Figs:** 31. **Type:** Cairns **Period:** Pre-Islamic (?) **MR 11**

There was a group of seven cairns 2 kms NW of Ghubba at the NW tip of a limestone ridge. They were interpreted as pre-Islamic burial mounds. They seemed to be circular structures/mounds to which stones had been added over time. All the cairns were similar, made from mounded sand with large (50-60 cms; 10 cms thick) and medium (20-30 cm) slabs of local beachstone.

Site MR 11.1 was large, measuring 20 m. x 8 m. x 2 m. high, with stretches of "walling" forming a facing. The rest varied in size, standing 1.5 m.-2 m. in height, although MR 11.5 was smaller, measuring 5 m. in diameter and it was only 50 cms. high. Site MR 11.7 seemed to be a satellite burial lying to the north of the main group of mounds.

Date: 16.4.92 **Figs:** 31. **Type:** Cairns **Period:** Pre-Islamic (?) **MR 12**

There were a group of at least six to seven cairns in a line along a ridge running N/S about 200 m. south of site MR 11. They were 1.5 m. in diameter and 40-50 cms high. They were made of local stone slabs (20 cms x 30 cms x 5 cms), piled to form low cairns.

Date: 15.4.92 **Figs:** 31. **Type:** Graveyard **Period:** Islamic **MR 13**

This site was an Islamic graveyard with about 100 burials (*ca* 20 children, of which five were probably for babies), lying to the north of Ghubba village at a distance of *ca* 1.5 km. - 2 km. east of Site 2. The graveyard lay on a bearing of 120° to site MR 4.8. The burial ground measured *ca* 20 m. x 40 m. The graves were large, measuring *ca* 2.5 m. x 1.2 m. and they had kerbs and head and foot stones, rising to 70 cms height. Their orientations vary slightly throughout the cemetery but average 246°-254°.

Three graves had headstones with holes which were possibly anchors. The cemetery was surprisingly far from the village, and we speculated that disease may explain this location. Many of the graves had an enamel teapot at their headstones, or on the grave itself. Occasionally, there was an enamel jug or basin instead, and two graves had ceramics scattered over them. One had a painted Julfâr-style (*i.e.* Late Islamic) vessel on it. Children's graves were concentrated in the southern area, and lacked such grave goods.

Plate 37. Late Islamic vessel on an Islamic period grave north of Ghubba (Site MR 13), Marawaḥ.

Notes

1 Brucks, *op. cit.*, p. 550-1.

2 See 1:250,000 "Ṣir Bani Yas, United Emirates", Series 1501, Sheet NG 39-16, edition 5-GSGS (1982 revised), Director of Military Survey, MOD, London; or the more accessible *United Arab Emirates*, 1:500,000, prepared by BP Exploration for the Centre for Documentation Research, Cultural Foundation, Abu Dhabi (1989), on C55205.

3 J. Harburgh, *op. cit.*, Section III, p. 245.

4 *op. cit.*, pp. 181-2.

5 P. Hellyer (ed.), *The Natural History of Marawaḥ Island, Abu Dhabi, United Arab Emirates. An Interim Report prepared for H.E. Major General Sheikh Mohammed Bin Zayed Al Nahyan*, Emirates Natural History Group, Abu Dhabi (June, 1990), pp. 3-4.

LIFFIYA (F)

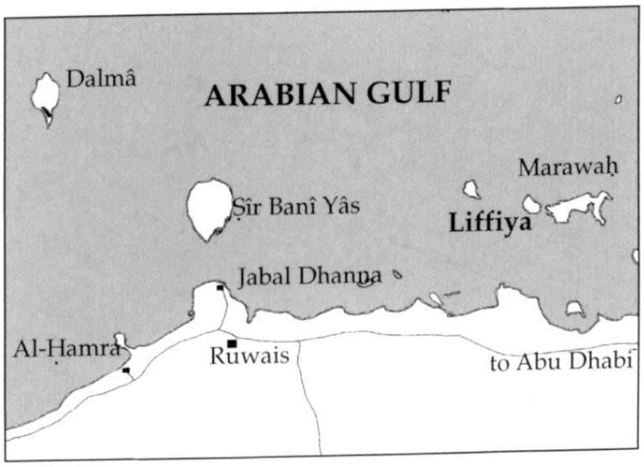

Liffiya (or al-Fiyya) was a small island off the NW end of Marawaḥ, opposite the village of Liffa[1]. It was separated by a short stretch of water[2]. There was a small village on the eastern shore known as Liffiya, with a landing beach nearby. Several people were living there at the time of the team's visit.

The southern and western coast was sandy with mangrove stands. In the middle of the western side was a *sabkha* filled inlet. The higher ground was formed by a limestone platform which constituted the terrain of the centre and north of the island.

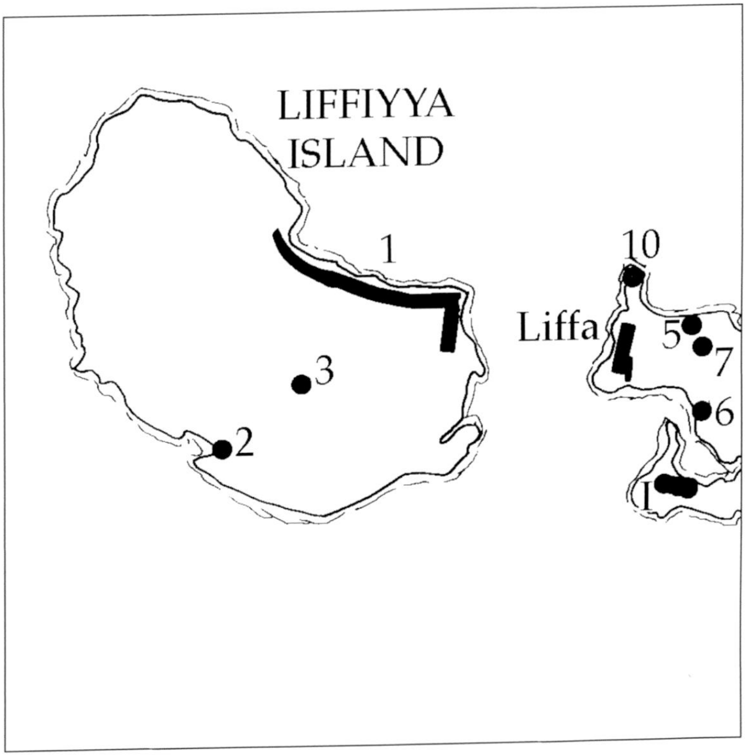

Fig. 33.
Liffiya site location.

Date: 13.4.92 **Figs:** 33. **Type:** Occupation **Period:** Late Islamic **F 1.1**

Site F 1.1 was an extended village on the east side of the island, running along the beach. The landing beach was at the SE end of the village. The shacks were made of plywood and hardboard on frames. Among refuse, there was shell near the foreshore.

F 1.2 **Date:** **Figs:** 33. **Type:** Occupation **Period:** Late Islamic (?)

This site was situated at the SE end of the village F 1.1, beside the landing beach. It consisted of the ruins of stone buildings. There were no ceramics but there was an overall scatter of shell.

F 1.3 **Date:** 13.4.92 **Figs:** 33. **Type:** Mosque **Period:** Late Islamic

This mosque, which was still in use, was built of stone and whitewashed. It measured 10 m. x 4.5 m. and it was oriented to *qibla* at 268°. There was a single entrance on axis with the centrally located *miḥrâb,* an arched,

Plate 38. Miḥrâb *of a mosque (F 1.3) on Liffiya.*

Plate 39. A mosque (F 1.3) on Liffiya.

curved recess 1 m. wide and forming a 1.5 m. projection on the exterior of the *qibla* wall. There were blind niches set into the inner surfaces of the walls.

To the east of the building was a courtyard measuring 7 m. x 12 m., outlined by rubble and entered from the east. Posts provided support for a covered area in front of the entrance to the prayer hall.

On the south side of the mosque was a dry-stone building that was described as a *Qur'ân* school. It measured 8 m. x 4.5 m. but was in poor repair.

Date: 13.4.92 **Figs:** 33. **Type:** Graveyard **Period:** Late Islamic

F 1.4

This site was a small graveyard with about 20 small graves (probably for children). It lay to the south of the village and west of Site F 1.2. It was of recent date.

Date: 13.4.92 **Figs:** 33. **Type:** Open Mosque **Period:** Late Islamic

F 1.5

This site was located NW of site F 1.3 and east of F 1.6. It was an open mosque comparable to sites SBY 10 and MR 5. It was built of large slabs of stone, on average 1 m.[2], with some 1.5 m. long or more: these were all set on edge to form walls and a *miḥrâb*. The mosque measured 9 m. x 3 m. with a single opening opposite the central *miḥrâb* which was in the form of a rectangular recess, measuring 1 m. x 1 m. The floor surface was of sand, except in front of the *miḥrâb* where there was matting.

Plate 40. A mosque at Liffiya (F 1.5).

F 1.6 **Date:** 13.4.92 **Figs:** 33. **Type:** Graveyard **Period:** Late Islamic

This graveyard was a roped off area on level sandy ground west of F 1.5 and *ca* 200 m. south of the shore. There were approximately 22 graves.

F 1.7 **Date:** 13.4.92 **Figs:** 33. **Type:** Occupation **Period:** Late Islamic

This was the north-west area of the the village of Liffiya. There were stone-built structures, including rectangular enclosures measuring 4.5 m. x 3 m. and a small rectangular cistern. The cistern measured 50 cms. x 40 cms and it was made of upright stone slabs. There were scatters of pottery, glass, shell and bone.

F 1.8 **Date:** 13.4.92 **Figs:** 33. **Type:** Mosque **Period:** Late Islamic

Site F 1.8 was an open air mosque built with medium-large flat stones slabs set on edge to form the *miḥrâb* and with small irregular stones for the other walls. The *qibla* wall was 6 m. long with a rectangular *miḥrâb* forming a 1 $m.^2$ projection, oriented to 260˚. Nowhere were the walls preserved to more than 80 cms height.

Plate 41. A mosque at Liffiya (F 1.8).

Date: 13.4.92 **Figs:** 33. **Type:** Butchery site **Period:** Late Islamic (?) **F 1.9**

This was a dugong butchery site, measuring some 5 m.[2] covered in dugong bones. It was on the sandy covered stone plateau to the SE of site F 1.8, *ca* 25 m. from the shore edge.

Date: 13.4.92 **Figs:** 33. **Type:** Midden **Period:** Late Islamic (?) **F 1.10**

This was a midden on the shore, SE of mosque F 1.8, measuring 10 m. x 5 m. with pearl oyster shells heavily represented.

Date: 13.4.92 **Figs:** 33. **Type:** Occupation **Period:** Islamic (?) **F 2.1**

This site lay in the SW part of island, to the east of the silted bay, where there was an area of natural limestone ridging, representing an earlier foreshore. On a flat area there were stone built structural remains covering an area 200 m. x 100 m. These included two to three collapsed circular and rectangular stone cairns and a small rectangular stone-lined cistern. No artefacts were found.

Date: 13.4.92 **Figs:** 33. **Type:** Cairns **Period:** ? **F 2.2-2.3**

These two sites were at the SW point of the island. They included two larger stone cairns both topped with more recent stones, possibly falcon perches. The low rectangular cairns were *ca* 2 m. x 4 m. There were also rectangular cisterns measuring 1.5 m. x 1 m. These were similar to F 1.2 and F 1.7 on the north side of Liffiya. The purpose of F 2.2 and 2.3 was not known by the present inhabitants of Liffiya.

F 3 **Date:** 13.4.92 **Figs:** 33. **Type:** Cairns **Period:** ?

This was an oval cairn measuring 5 m. x 3 m. and between 0.5 m. to 1 m. high, situated on a low ridge on the west side of the island near the *sabkha*.

Notes

1. Pronunciation is often near to "Fîyeh".
2. A short visit by boat was made on 13th April, 1992. Team members who went to Liffiya included B. de Cardi, R.L. Stocks, J.L. Wucher King, and Eid al-Mazruʿî. The team was driven on Liffîya by Khamîs b. Khalîfa b. Naym al-Rumaythî.

SURFACE FINDS

THE LITHICS AND CERAMICS RETRIEVED in the course of the season were the principal indicators for dating the sites examined on Ṣîr Banî Yâs, Dalmâ and Marawaḥ. Inscriptions were rare although some late Islamic inscriptions were found. No coins were found during the survey.

The most notable early sites were DA 11 and DA 12 on Dalmâ and MR 1 on Marawaḥ. The attribution of DA 11 and 12 as ᶜUbaid-related is based on the presence of painted ᶜUbaid ware, dated to *ca* 6000-7000 BP (Plate 44). At DA 11, there were also weights, beads and lithics which appeared to be associated with the ᶜUbaid finds (Plates 45, 46)[1]. This was the first ᶜUbaid pottery reported from Abu Dhabi although ᶜUbaid sites are known further east in the UAE in Ajman[2], Umm al-Quwain[3] and Ra's al-Khaimah. The presence of numerous wells at Dalmâ made it one of the most attractive places for settlement in the coastal area and this would have ensured that the island was the scene of human activity.

The lithics from Site MR 1 at Marawaḥ suggest a date of *ca* 6000 BP and are related to the Arabian Bifacial Tradition (Plates 52, 53, 54): they were particularly numerous and lay scattered around possible structural remains. From the same period is a tile knife from SBY 24 at Ra's Danân on the north end of Ṣîr Banî Yâs.

Thereafter, there appears to have been a long hiatus on all three islands until the 1st millenium AD. Even though a 2nd-3rd millennium BC site was identified on Ṣîr Banî Yâs in the second season of the project (1993), the fact remains that so far there is a paucity of sites of Bronze Age date on these islands. However, bulldozing and plantation on Ṣîr Banî Yâs and Dalmâ has been so extensive that the absence of sites of this period merely may reflect site loss in recent years.

The 1st millennium AD is well represented on Ṣîr Banî Yâs where Sites SBY 1 - SBY 9 all have significant amounts of *ca* 6th-7th century pottery, including blue glazed wares and fine unglazed wares (Plate 42). The moulded plaster (Figs 10-13; Plate 10) found on the surface at SBY 9 fits well with this dating.

There are also wares of the same 1st millenium AD date on Dalmâ at DA 7. This is one of the most important sites on the island inasmuch as the Islamic graveyard preserves intact the integrity of the archaeological context as it was before Dalmâ was transformed by modern development projects. The ceramics found at the graveyard span the period *ca* 6th-7th century AD through the middle Islamic period to the Late Islamic period.

The discovery of finds indicating settlement on Ṣîr Banî Yâs and Dalmâ in the years immediately preceding Islam and in the early Islamic period should be seen in the context of 1st millenium AD settlement along the Qatar coast[4]; from the *ca* 1st-4th centuries AD from ed-Dûr (Umm al-

Quwain)[5] and Mleiha (al-Milayḥa) in Sharjah[6]; from the pre-Islamic to early Abbasid period at al-Jumayra in Sharjah[7]; from *ca* 3rd century AD to early, middle and late Islamic at al-Ḥulayla, Ra's al-Khaimah[8]; and from the 1st millennium AD at al-Khaṭṭ, Ra's al-Khaimah[9]. It is into this broader evidence of 1st millennium AD settlement patterns in the UAE and elsewhere that the Ṣîr Banî Yâs and Dalmâ sites eventually will have to be placed.

The middle Islamic period on the islands examined appears to be poorly represented. However, DA 7, the Islamic graveyard on Dalmâ, preserves evidence of 14th century activity, indicated by Longquan celadons (Plates 43, 50, 51) and by fritware sherds and inscribed blue-glazed ware from Iran (Plates 47, 48, 49).

As everywhere in the area, the later Islamic period is extremely well represented, with numerous sites with ceramics parallelling the Julfâr horizon[10]. Ceramics of the post-14th to 19th centuries and beyond are widely encountered on Ṣîr Banî Yâs, Dalmâ and Marawaḥ. This evidence of activity and settlement confirms locally held perceptions in Abu Dhabi, suggesting that, until the relatively recent past, there was a considerable population on the off-shore islands. The old fishing and pearling industries were intimately related to this past occupation of the islands. Among other factors explaining their present state is the decline of the pearling industry in the early 20th century. Since then, modern development after the discovery of oil has completely changed the historical settlement pattern of the entire region, and has attracted people to the modern towns of the UAE.

Plate 42. Ceramics from the ca 6th-7th C. A.D. sites at Ṣîr Banî Yâs.

Plate 43. Chinese celadon and blue and white porcelain from Dalmâ (DA 7).

Plate 44. Ceramics and ceramic weight from the ʿUbaid-related site at Dalmâ (DA 11).

Plate 45. Beads from the ʿUbaid related site at Dalmâ (DA 11).

Plate 46. Lithics from the ʿUbaid related site at Dalmâ (DA 11).

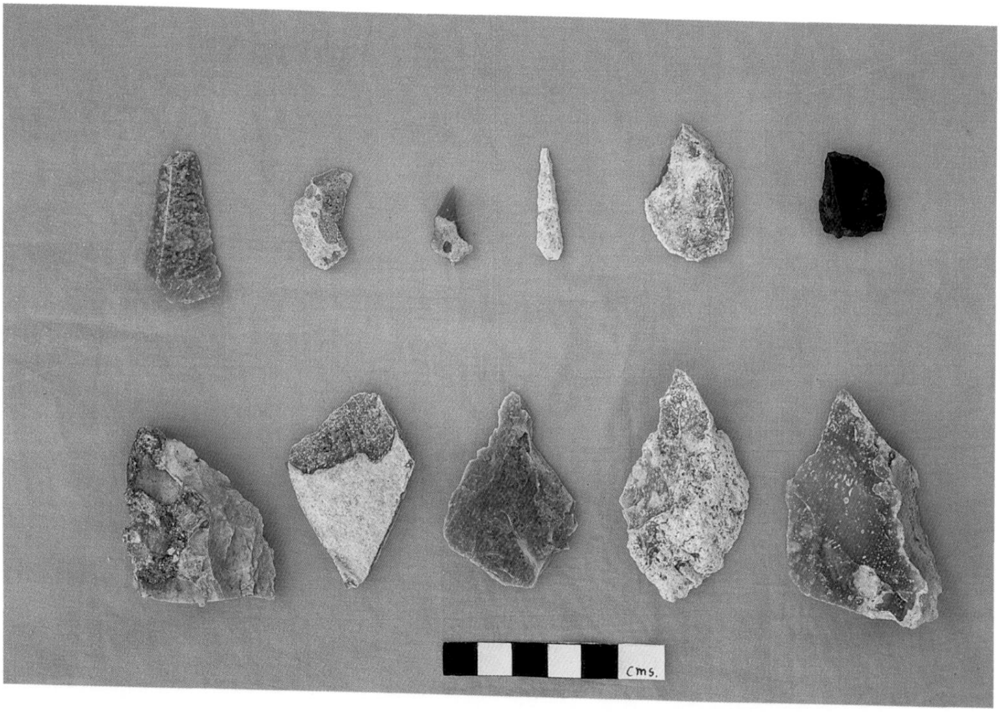

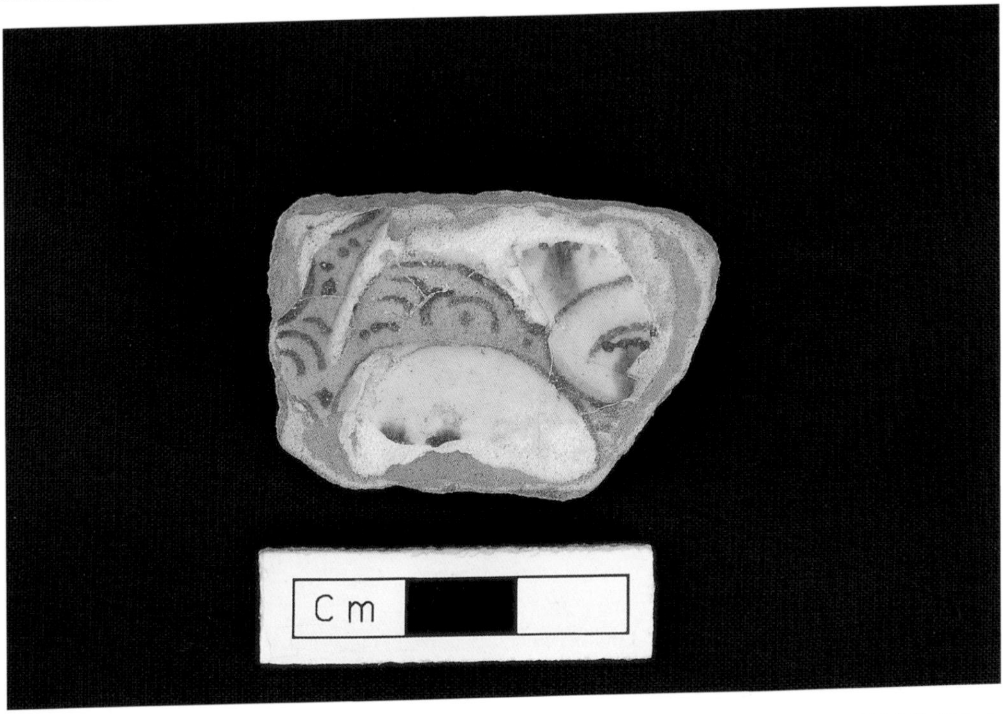

Plate 47. Fritware imported from Iran (14th C.), from an Islamic graveyard (DA 7), Dalmâ.

Plate 48. Fritware imported from Iran (14th C.), from an Islamic graveyard (DA 7), Dalmâ.

Plate 49. Inscribed glazed ware imported from Iran, from an Islamic graveyard (DA 7), Dalmâ.

Plate 50. Longquan celadon (14th C.), from an Islamic graveyard (DA 7), Dalmâ.

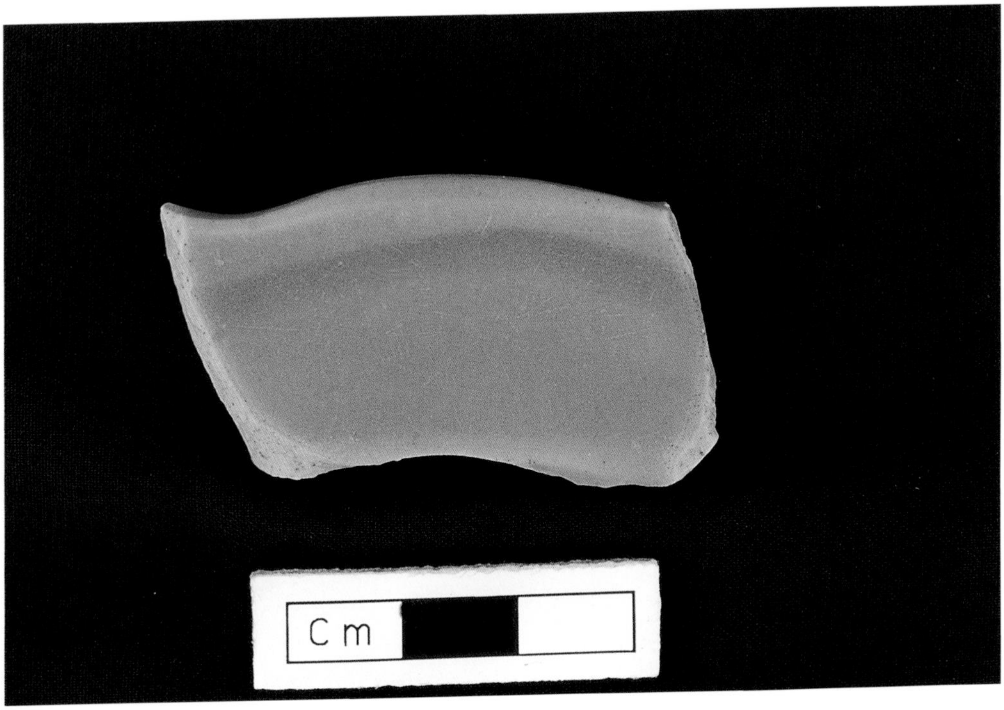

Plate 51. Longquan celadon (14th C.), from an Islamic graveyard (DA 7), Dalmâ.

Plate 52. Late Stone Age lithics (Site MR 1), Marawaḥ.

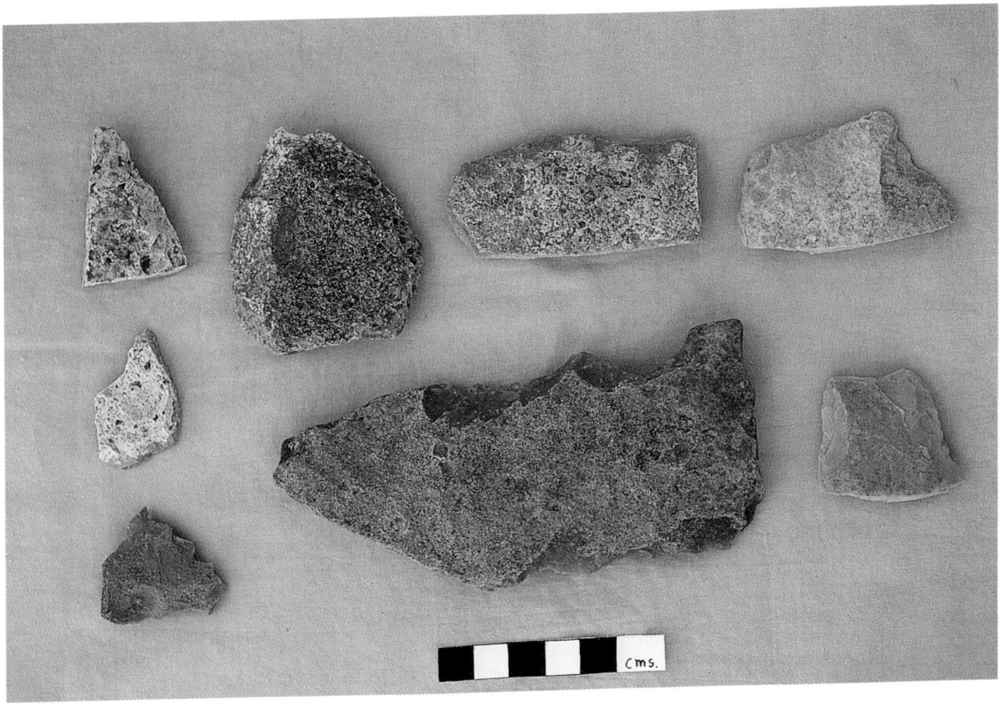

Plate 53. Late Stone Age lithic (Site MR 1), Marawaḥ.

Plate 54. Late Stone Age arrow head (Site MR 1), Marawaḥ, Arabian Bifacial Tradition.

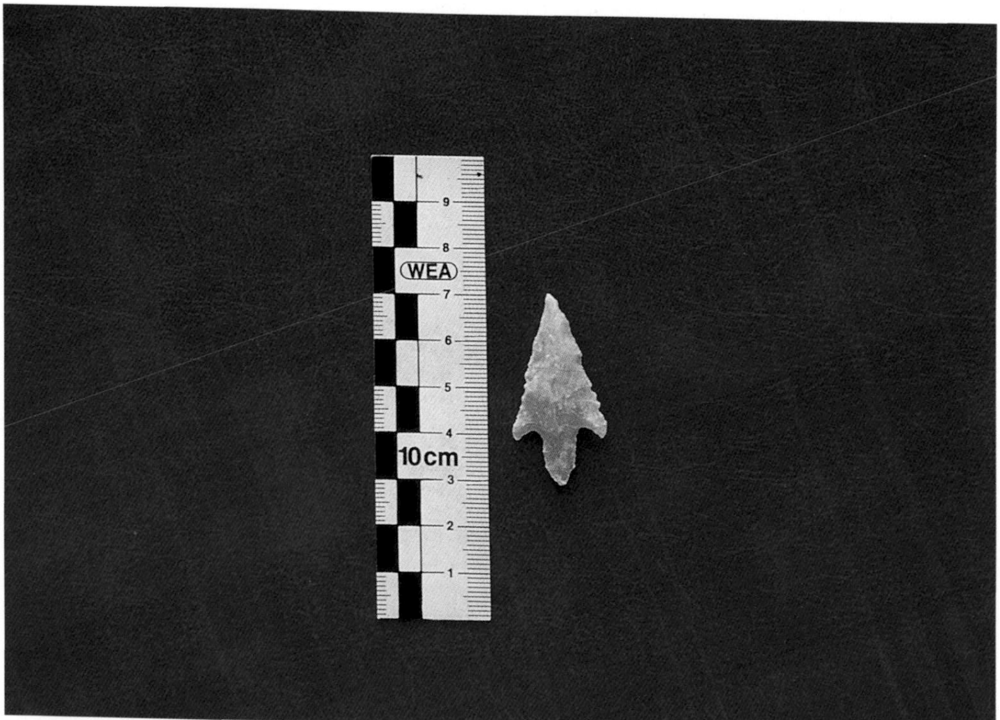

NOTES

1 Subsequent excavations at the site by the ADIAS team are reported by Katelin Flavin and Elizabeth Shepherd, "Fishing in the Gulf: Preliminary Investigations at an Ubaid site, Dalma (UAE)", *Proceedings of the Seminar for Arabian Studies* 24 (1994), pp. 115-134.

2 M. Millet, "Comments on the lithic material from an 'Ubaid site in the Emirate of Ajman (U.A.E.), *Arabian Archaeology and Epigraphy* 2 (1991), pp. 91-2.
E. Haerinck, "Heading for the Straits of Hormuz, an 'Ubaid site in the Emirate of Ajman (U.A.E.)"
Arabian Archaeology and Epigraphy 2 (1991), pp. 91-2.

3 R. Boucharlat, E. Haerinck, C.S. Phillips and D.T. Potts, "Note on the Ubaid-pottery site in the Emirate of Umm al-Quwain", *Arabian Archaeology and Epigraphy* 2 (1991), pp. 84-90.

4 B. de Cardi, *op. cit.*, pp. 185-6.
C. Hardy-Guilbert, "Fouilles archaeologiques à Murwab, Qatar", in R. Boucharlat and J.F. Salles (eds), *Arabie orientale, Mesopotamie et Iran meridionale de l'age du fer au debut de la periode islamique (Reunion de travail, Lyon, 1982)*, Paris (1984), pp. 169-188.
C. Hardy-Guilbert, "Dix ans de recherche archéologique sur la periode islamique dans le golfe (1977-19870", *Documents de l'Islam medieval. Nouvelles Perspectives de Recherche, Actes de la Table Ronde*, CNRS, Paris (3-5 mars 1988)(1991), pp. 134-140.

5 Potts, *op. cit.*ii, pp. 274-291.

6 M. Mouton, *Le Peninsule d'Oman de la Fin de l'Age du fer au Debut de la Periode sassanide (25- av. -350 ap. JC)*; i, Paris (1992). Unpublished Thèse de Doctorat, Université de Paris I (Pantheon-Sorbonne).

7 D.C. Baramki, "An Ancient Caravan Station in Dubai", *Illustrated London News*, 2903 (1975).

8 D. Kennet and G.R.D. King, "Jazîrat al-Ḥulayla-early Julfâr", *Journal of the Royal Asiatic Society*, 3rd series, vol. 4, part 2 (July, 1994), pp. 163-212.

9 B. de Cardi, D. Kennet and R.L. Stocks, "Five Thousand Years of Settlement at Khatt, UAE", *Proceedings of the Seminar for Arabian Studies* 24 (1994), pp. 53-61.

10 J. Hansman, *Julfâr, An Arabian Port*, London (1985), pp. 68-75.

BIBLIOGRAPHY

D.C. Baramki, "An Ancient Caravan Station in Dubai", *Illustrated London News*, 2903 (1975).

J. Beaucamp and C. Robin, "L'évêque nestorien de Masmahig dans l'archipel d'al-Bahrain", in *Dilmun. New Studies in the Archaeology and early History of Bahrain*, ed. D. Potts, Berlin (1983), pp.181-196.

R. Boucharlat, E. Haerinck, C.S. Phillips and D.T. Potts, "Note on the Ubaid-pottery site in the Emirate of Umm al-Quwain", *Arabian Archaeology and Epigraphy* 2 (1991), pp. 84-90.

J.S. Buckingham, *Travels in Assyria, Media, and Persia*, London (1829).

B. de Cardi, *Qatar Archaeological Report. Excavations 1973*, Oxford (1978).

B. de Cardi, D. Kennet and R.L. Stocks, "Five Thousand Years of Settlement at Khatt, UAE", *Proceedings of the Seminar for Arabian Studies* 24 (1994), pp. 53-61).

W. Facey, "The Boat Carvings at Jabal Jusasiyya, N.E. Qatar", *Proceedings of the Seminar for Arabian Studies* 17 (1987), pp. 199-222.

K. Flavin and E. Shepherd, "Fishing in the Gulf: Preliminary Investigations at an Ubaid site, Dalma (UAE)", *Proceedings of the Seminar for Arabian Studies* 24 (1994), pp. 115-134.

E. Haerinck, "Heading for the Straits of Hormuz, an 'Ubaid site in the Emirate of Ajman (U.A.E.)", *Arabian Archaeology and Epigraphy* 2 (1991), pp. 84-90.

J. Hansman, *Julfâr, An Arabian Port*, London (1985).

G. Harter, S. Cleuziou, J.P. Laffont, J. Nockin and R. Toussaint, *Emirat d'Abu Dhabi. Propositions pour Dalma*, (Sept.-Oct., 1979).

C. Hardy-Guilbert, "Fouilles archaeologiques à Murwab, Qatar", in R. Boucharlat and J.F. Salles, eds., *Arabie orientale, Mesopotamie et Iran meridional de l'age du fer au debut de la periode islamique* (Reunion de travail, Lyon, 1982), Paris (1984), pp. 169-188.

C. Hardy-Guilbert, "Dix ans de récherche archéologique sur la period islamique dans le Golfe (1977-1987)", *Documents de l'Islam medieval. Nouvelles Perspectives de Recherche, Actes de la Table Ronde*, CNRS, Paris (3-5 mars 1988) (1991), 131-192.

P. Hellyer (ed.), *The Natural History of Merawah Island, Abu Dhabi, United Arab Emirates. An Interim Report prepared for H.E. Major General Sheikh Mohammed Bin Zayed Al Nahyan*, Emirates Natural History Group, Abu Dhabi (June, 1990).

D. Kennet and G.R.D. King, "Jazîrat al-Ḥulayla-early Julfâr", *Journal of the Royal Asiatic Society*, 3rd series, vol. 4, part 2 (July, 1994), pp. 163-212.

G.R.D. King, *The Islamic Architecture of Dalma, Abu Dhabi, United Arab Emirates* (at press).

G.R.D. King, D. Dunlop, J. Elders, S. Garfi, A. Stephenson and C. Tonghini, "A Report on the Abu Dhabi Islands Archaeological Survey (1993-4)", *Proceedings of the Seminar for Arabian Studies* 25 (1995), pp. 63-74.

D. Lee, *Flight from the Middle East. A History of the Royal Air Force in the Arabian Peninsula and adjacent territories 1945-1972*, London (1980).

C. Lehmann, "Pottery Sherds, Sir Bani Yas, 2-3 May, 1991", unpublished report.

S. McBrearty, "Lithic artifacts from Abu Dhabi's Western Region", *Tribulus, Bulletin of the Emirates Natural History Group* (1993), 3.1, pp. 13-14.

C. C. Mann, *Abu Dhabi: Birth of an Oil Shaikhdom*, Beirut (1969).

M. Millet, "Comments on the lithic material from an 'Ubaid site in the Emirate of Ajman (U.A.E.)", *Arabian Archaeology and Epigraphy* 2 (1991), pp. 91-92.

M. Mouton, *La Peninsule d'Oman de la Fin de l'Age du Fer au Debut de la Periode Sassanide (25- av.-350 ap. JC)*, Paris (1992). Unpublished Thèse de Doctorat, Universite de Paris I (Pantheon-Sorbonne).

Persian Gulf Pilot comprising the Persian Gulf and its approaches, from Ras al Hadd, in the south-west, to Cape Monze, in the East, 8th ed., London (1932).

D.T. Potts, *The Arabian Gulf in Antiquity*, Oxford (1990; 1992), 2 vols.

B.J. Slot, *The Arabs of the Gulf, 1602-1784. An alternative approach to the early history of the Arab Gulf States and the Arab peoples of the Gulf, mainly based on sources of the Dutch East India Company*, Leidschenden (1993).

Freya Stark, *The Coast of Incense. Autobiography, 1933-1939*, London (1953).

Captain Robert Taylor, "The Persian Gulf", in "Extracts from brief notes, containing historical and other information connected with the Province of Oman; Muskat and the adjoining country; the islands of Bahrein, Ormus, Kishm, and Karrack; and other ports and places in the Persian Gulf", Bombay (1818), in *Selections from the Records of the Bombay Government*, no. xxix, New Series, Bombay (1856), pp. 16-17.

W. Tikritî, "Al-masâḥ al-athârî fî'l-mantiqat al-gharbîya min imârat Abû Ẓabî", *Archaeology in the United Arab Emirates* V (1989), pp. 9-19 (Arabic section).

B. Vogt, W. Gockel, H. Hofbauer and A.A. al-Haj, "The Coastal Survey in the Western Province of Abu Dhabi, 1983", *Archaeology in the United Arab Emirates* V (1989), p. 49-60.

D. Whitehouse, "Excavations at Sirâf", *Iran* x (1972), pp. 74-75.

P. J. Whybrow, "New stratotype; the Baynunah Formation (Late Miocene), United Arab Emirates: lithology and palaeontology", *Newsletter of Stratigraphy*, 21 (1989), pp. 1-9.

P.J. Whybrow, A. Hill, W.Y. Tikriti and E.A. Hailwood, "Late Miocene primate fauna, flora and initial palaeomagnetic date from the Emirate of Abu Dhabi, United Arab Emirates", *Journal of Human Evolution* 19 (1990), pp. 583-588.

P.J. Whybrow, A. Hill, W.Y. Tikriti and E.A. Hailwood, "Miocene fossils from Abu Dhabi", *Tribulus, Bulletin of the Emirates Natural History Group* (1991), 1.1, pp. 4-9.